VAIDEOL
by Steve Vai

All illustrations by Steve Vai

ISBN 978-1-5400-3099-3

HAL•LEONARD®

Copyright © 2019 SyVy Music (ASCAP)
International Copyright Secured All Rights Reserved

Visit Hal Leonard Online at
www.halleonard.com

Contact us:
Hal Leonard
7777 West Bluemound Road
Milwaukee, WI 53213
Email: info@halleonard.com

In Europe, contact:
Hal Leonard Europe Limited
42 Wigmore Street
Marylebone, London, W1U 2RN
Email: info@halleonardeurope.com

In Australia, contact:
Hal Leonard Australia Pty. Ltd.
4 Lentara Court
Cheltenham, Victoria, 3192 Australia
Email: info@halleonard.com.au

CONTENTS

ACKNOWLEDGMENTS

Big thanks go to all the phenomenal music and life mentors I've had throughout my career: Bill Westcott, Joe Satriani, Wes Hensel, Joe Bell, Mike Metheny, Frank Zappa, and David Lee Roth.

And sincere thanks to all the "campers" that have joined the Vai Academy retreats. I learn so much from all of you, and this document was originally written for you.

Thanks also to Jason Henke for his editing, Jay Graydon for his insight, and special thanks to Cory McCormick for finding all my errors.

INTRODUCTION

In short…
This document is a guide to the fundamentals of music theory for the aspiring guitar player.

In long…
Do you need to know music theory to be a good musician? That's one of the commonly asked questions I hear when speaking to aspiring guitarists. It seems to be a source of confusion and concern for many. Here's something to ponder: whatever you are interested in, you will naturally seek out to understand because you are *interested* in it. If you find yourself fascinated with understanding the language of music, nothing will stop you from seeking it out and making it part of your musical vocabulary.

But, if you are not interested in understanding music theory, chances are, you will struggle through the tedious process of employing discipline and memorizing things that may eventually be only nominally helpful at best. The good news is that it's not the academics of music that will make you an effective musician; of vital importance is your creative imagination and your enthusiasm for a good idea. Perhaps the most powerful connective tool to your instrument is the quality of your inner musical ear. This is what manifests the invisible into the physical.

There are many who couldn't care less about knowing anything regarding the academics of music, but are powerful music creators nonetheless (I refer to music theory and technique as the "academics" of music).

Then there are those who have a strong desire to master the language of music, but the whole process seems overwhelming and intimidating. And some may even feel embarrassed that they are virtually musically illiterate and have a quiet but insidious belief in their head that they just aren't smart enough to comprehend it. Whatever you believe will be true to you… until you change your mind about it.

Some people can be very critical and may tell you that, if you understand music theory, it will compromise your ability to "play from the heart." I would recommend not buying into that premise. This may or may not be the case. The trick is in finding the balance.

And some people may start to study the language of music and realize its vast hidden potential in unlocking deep creativity in their musical imagination; they discover that it's not that complicated at all, it makes sense, and feels very natural to them with a little study. They start to see the infinite creativity it allows, in ways that not understanding music would never be able to unlock. In this case, it's not uncommon to develop a voracious appetite for the study of music theory. It's all good.

The question is: What do you want?

Everybody has a different set of desires and abilities in understanding things at various levels. Some people are more intellectual thinkers than artistic thinkers, and that's fine. You can always choose to develop your skills in various areas that are not natural to you, but a good rule of thumb is to follow your enthusiasm exclusively.

"Follow Your Bliss" – Joseph Campbell

If a very intellectually gifted person absorbs the depths of music theory, they may find themselves creating complex theoretical music for the sake of fascinating themselves with their own intellect. The music they create may inevitably sound like… well, meandering intellectualized exercises. *And that's fine, too*, if that's what they want to do. There's creative artistic value in that for some listeners, and, if it's fulfilling for the composers, it's a win-win.

Since as far back as I can remember remembering, I always had a deep fascination with the written language of music. On paper, it looked like beautiful art to me. It felt like a warm, safe place (a bizarre analogy, I know). It was this mysterious language that I instinctively knew could unlock my musical expressions. To be able to write a composition for a large group of people by starting with a blank piece of score paper, with its infinite possibilities for inventiveness, was absolutely spellbinding to me. I always had an intense desire to understand it fully and master it completely. Although I'm still a work in progress—because the evolution of music theory is infinite—I so much enjoy being able to use what I do know, and I still continue to study it.

Besides taking up the accordion at nine years of age (just like all good Italian boys from Long Island), my serious studies in music theory started in seventh grade, when I took a music theory class that was taught by a guy who I considered brilliant: Bill Westcott. This is where I learned the fundamentals and much more. It wasn't until I met Joe Satriani when I was 12 years old and started taking guitar lessons with him that I began to understand how to apply this music theory to the guitar to unlock some of its mysteries, as compared to composing for various players. Joe took the same theory classes with Bill as I did, perhaps four years or so before me. Although Joe possesses a high degree of intellect and musical understanding, his inner melodious heart uses music theory to do his inspired bidding.

When I attended Berklee College of Music after high school, I was able to delve more into the study of music theory, particularly in the jazz idiom, and classes with Wes Hensel and Mike Metheny were very helpful. My attraction to the music of Frank Zappa was supreme because in him I saw it all being done the way I always wanted to do it, but perhaps with different notes. Frank used everything and anything to get his point across, and he reached into the depth—and beyond—of any of the available elements at his disposal, be it composition, guitar playing, technology, humor, etc.

Intellectual Understanding vs. Experiential Knowing

You will notice in the examples in this book, I stress taking what you are learning to a deeper level than just the intellectual understanding of it. By going deeper, I am referring to making it **experiential**. There is a vast difference between memorizing something and understanding it intellectually and knowing something "experientially."

An analogy of this might be found in honey. You can learn what honey is on an intellectual level. You can be a specialist on the properties of it and even be the world's leading authority on it. You can write volumes of information about honey, explaining its origin, molecular structure, how it's made, all the different varieties, etc., and you can even give exhaustive and imaginative explanations on what it tastes like. But a person will never actually know what honey really is until they put it in their mouth and focus on the flavor of it, because the taste of honey is experiential and has virtually nothing to do with the intellectual understanding of it.

In the learning and utilization of the academics of music, the intellectual understanding of it has its place. In any field, there is a period that a person goes through when they need to hone their vessel, so to speak. You need to apply your focus to the learning of the modality for a while, but the most effective method of "owning" what you are learning is to evolve past the learning by making it second nature, with no real need to think about it. It just becomes a "knowing" that does not require thinking. And in order for that to happen, one needs to have evolved the learning into the experiential knowing stage. Geez, I hope this makes sense… I'm trying.

One of the secrets to achieving this is in your ability to listen with great intensity to whatever it is you are learning or playing. When you play what you are learning, it becomes tangible in a different way than just as a thought. When listening intensely, you are not thinking; you are instead being present. Being present is a higher state than thinking.

The importance of listening to what you are playing cannot be stressed enough, and there are various exercises for listening on a deeper level throughout this book.

So, to know music theory or not? If that is the question, my answer might be: it doesn't matter, but what matters more are your interests and desires. Having said that, I always recommend at least a basic understanding of the fundamentals of music theory, and, since I'm primarily a guitar player, I decided to create this book, which I believe covers those simple fundamentals and how to apply them to the guitar. I believe these academics are relatively simple to understand but can greatly aid your understanding of the basic language of music. This will inevitably make your songwriting, communication with other musicians, and navigation on the instrument easier and more effective. It can also inspire you to create and express certain musical ideas that you may not have had access to if you were completely musically illiterate.

This book is not meant to be a guitar lesson, per se, but more of a document on basic music theory. The lines blur at times, but a guitar lesson-type book would include much more of a focus on technique.

In this book, I've tried to give the basics as they may apply to a guitar player, but I also touch on some advanced concepts that you can explore if interested. I might recommend taking the time to completely read through this document twice and just see what pieces to the puzzle immediately come together. But in the real learning and memorization aspects of this book, I might suggest going one subject at a time until you have mastered it, then move on to the next subject—even if it takes a week or more for each subject. This book is constructed in chronological order, so once each section is mastered, the next should make sense.

If you find yourself fascinated with music theory, there are myriad opportunities to deepen your understandings. And these days, with the Internet, they are at your fingertips.

The idea is to take the path of least resistance; that is, look into yourself and go with whatever it is that feels natural and instinctual to you, regardless of what anybody says you should do.

If you are not interested in having a basic understanding of the academics of music, then throw this book away and move on. But, if you do desire to have a handle on music theory, then read on.

In closing, I would say that it's important to understand that wherever you're at right now in your understanding of music theory or technical development as a player is just fine, and wherever you decide you want to go with it is just fine, too.

Everything is just fine. As a matter of fact, it's infinitely better than just fine; it's intensely phenomenal. Hey, you're playing the guitar!

Enjoy,
Steve Vai
December 10, 2017, 3:04pm
Pune, India

NOTES ON THE NECK
(ACADEMIC STUDY)

Make the rest of your life with the guitar a little easier by memorizing every note on the neck, cold! Even the ones you may not be using much. Take the time and just memorize them all perfectly.

There are some excellent apps and diagrams online that can help and that you may want to check out. Just search online for "Guitar Fretboard Notes" or anything like that.

Here are some basic points to understand:

- In conventional Western music, there are 12 notes in the equal temperament system. These notes create the **chromatic scale** and repeat themselves, low to high (or vice versa).

- In the chromatic scale, the 12 notes are a **half step** apart from each other. A half step is also known as a **semitone**. On the guitar, a half step is the distance from one fret to the next, either lower or higher. A **whole step** is the distance of two frets.

- The natural notes in music are C, D, E, F, G, A, and B.

Accidentals

An **accidental** is a symbol that indicates if a note is to be played in its natural state or raised or lowered in various degrees.

♯ This is the **sharp** symbol. It raises the note one half step (e.g., C♯).

♭ This is the **flat** symbol. It lowers the note one half step (e.g., B♭).

♮ This is the **natural** symbol. It indicates that the note it is representing is played in its natural state (e.g., C♮). This symbol overrides any sharps or flats that were applied to the same note earlier in the bar of music. It also indicates that any of the same notes after it would be played in their natural position. If an accidental appears on a particular tone in a bar of music, that accidental does not affect the same note in the bar if the note is played in a different octave.

𝄪 This is the **double sharp** symbol. It raises the note one whole step (two frets).

𝄫 This is the **double flat** symbol. It lowers the note one whole step (two frets).

Enharmonic Tones

Enharmonic tones are notes that can have several names but are actually the same tone, such as C♯ and D♭.

F𝄪, G♮, and A♭♭ are actually all the same note; that is, they are enharmonic tones.

Below is a diagram of the neck of the guitar with all the notes color-coded, with enharmonic tones in a red circle. You will notice that B♯ is enharmonic to C♮, and E♯ is enharmonic to F♮. They are not included as enharmonic tones in this chart. The double fret markers on the 12th fret represent the octave, and from there, the notes repeat themselves. Be sure to memorize the notes on the neck past the 12th fret.

GUITAR FRETBOARD NOTES

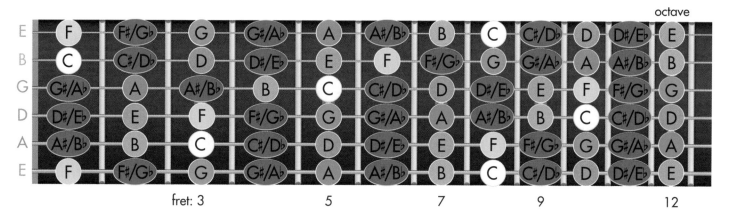

NOTES ON THE NECK (EXPERIENTIAL STUDY)

Listen Intensely

It's a good idea to memorize these notes so they are instantaneously recognized on the neck without having to think what they are. But there is a more powerful way to create a relationship with these notes than to just memorize their positions on the neck, and that's to listen intensely to the note beyond its name. Every note has somewhat of a different color, dimension, personality, emotional equilibrium, and story to it. These differences can seem very subtle, and most people do not consciously distinguish the differences, but may feel the differences subconsciously. Each person experiences the qualities of notes differently. What do they mean to you?

Take the time to give the note your full attention by just listening as deeply as you can and recognizing, on those subtle levels, how that note makes you feel. Merge your being with the name of the note, along with the personality, emotion, and color of the note. See how the notes differ in hue from one to another. In doing this, you are essentially creating an intimate relationship with each individual note.

This can aid you tremendously when it comes time to delve into your imagination to find melodies and chords that can best express your creative intentions. Chances are, you may have never learned to do this before. But, if you do this, you are taking the note from the intellectualized stage, which is the memorization of its position on the neck or any other information you can apply to it, to the experiential stage, which is the inner, intimate connection of the soul of the note's vibration and how it resounds with you.

This is a meditation of sorts, and the more you focus on the resonance of each note, the deeper your personal relationship with that note will be. By the way, the notes love it when you do this with them. They will start singing to you.

When you are listening deeply and memorizing the quality of the note itself, try using the part of your brain that you go to when you are memorizing something. Sort of as if someone was telling you their phone number, and you were trying to memorize it. You sort of take an audible picture of it in your mind's ear.

But make sure you have instant recognition of their names on the frets. Here is a great exercise that you can do for the intellectual learning of the note's position on the neck. Record yourself saying the phrases below, and when you listen back, play those notes on the guitar neck instantly. Go through it twice, once for the notes below the 12th fret, and once for the notes above it. Once you have a relatively good handle on this, re-record them, but only give yourself a half a second or less to find the note.

Whenever a note is requested on the E string, recognize the note on both E strings and also find the notes in both octaves on the given string.

NOTE RECOGNITION EXERCISE

E on E string	F♯ on A string	C on D string	F♭ on G string	G on G string
B♭ on G string	F♯ on E string	E♭ on D string	A on A string	E on B string
E♯ on E string	D♭ on D string	G♯ on A string	C♭ on B string	B♭ on B string
G on A string	F♭ on E string	B on D string	D♭ on G string	F♯ on B string
F on E string	F♭ on D string	G♭ on A string	B♯ on G string	A♯ on B string
B♭ on A string	D♯ on D string	E on G string	G♭ on B string	B♭ on E string
G♭ on E string	F♭ on A string	G on B string	C♭ on D string	C on G string
G♯ on B string	E♯ on A string	E♭ on E string	F♯ on D string	E♯ on G string
E♭ on B string	G on E string	C♯ on A string	G♯ on G string	G♯ on E string
G♭ on G string	A♭ on E string	B on A string	E on D string	C♯ on B string
D♭ on A string	A on E string	F♯ on G string	F♭ on B string	F on D string
A♯ on E string	E♯ on B string	G♭ on D string	F on A string	E♭ on G string
B on E string	G on D string	C♭ on A string	A on G string	D♯ on B string
B on B string	B♯ on E string	A♯ on A string	G♯ on D string	D♯ on G string
D on B string	E on A string	D♭ on E string	A♯ on D string	C♭ on G string
A♭ on A string	C♯ on D string	A on B string	B♯ on D string	D on G string
C♭ on E string	F on B string	D on A string	B♭ on D string	C♯ on G string
C on E string	C on A string	A on D string	A♯ on G string	A♭ on B string
D♯ on A string	D on D string	B on G string	C on B string	D on E string
A♭ on D string	C♯ on E string	B♯ on B string	B♯ on A string	A♭ on G string
D♯ on E string	E♯ on D string	F on G string	E♭ on A string	D♭ on B string

NOTES (ADVANCED)

Microtones

Microtones are notes that exist in between a half step (smaller than a semitone). These notes are also called **micro intervals**. Conventionally, between a half step there are 100 micro intervals, which are called **cents**. So, there are 100 cents within the span of a semitone, or half step. But, on the guitar, you would have to find them by bending the note slightly because these notes exist "in between" one fret (half step).

We will only concern ourselves here with **quarter tones**, which is the note that exists directly in between a half-step interval. A quarter tone is 50 cents sharp or flat. You may find various symbols used in microtonal music that represent the same note alteration. Below are the relatively common ones, and they are the ones I use.

‡ = ¼-tone sharp

♯ = ¾-tone sharp

♭ = ¼-tone flat

♭ = ¾-tone flat

If you venture into microtonal music, you may find a host of microtonal symbols that are used in various cultures or by various composers.

COMPREHENSIVE ACCIDENTALS LIST

Advanced Note Recognition

Of great importance for any musician is the development of their musical ear. This is at the core of the connection between your creative musical ideas and your fingers. Being born with a highly developed musical ear is quite a nice gift, but it's also possible to develop your ear. It will naturally develop in time through listening to music, imagining it, playing it, and sharing in the creation of it, etc.

There is a plethora of exercises and studies a person can do to develop his/her ear, and I would highly recommend engaging in any you can find or imagine. Here are some:

1. Sing what you play

2. Sing what you play in harmony (all scale degrees)

3. Listen to your favorite songs and try to figure them out

4. Memorize intervals by ear

5. Learn to sight-sing

6. Transcribe all sorts of music

Here's something to experiment with off the bat: take the previous Note Recognition Exercise (whereby you made a recording of the names of the notes in order to recognize them), but this time, first play the note, leave a few seconds or less, and then name the note with your voice. When listening back, see if you can name the note just by hearing the quality of it. Naming the string on which the note is being played is unnecessary. Just listen deeply to the note and see if you can identify its pitch. You may discover that you have perfect pitch!

SCALES (ACADEMIC STUDY)

There are many ways to approach scales, but I'm going to outline the way I learned them on the guitar when I was a youngster.

For me, there were four main scales. In particular, the blues scale was most important, and I'll explain why when we get to modes.

1. Major

2. Minor

3. Pentatonic

4. Blues

This is the G major scale in second position. Its modal name is **Ionian**.

G MAJOR SCALE

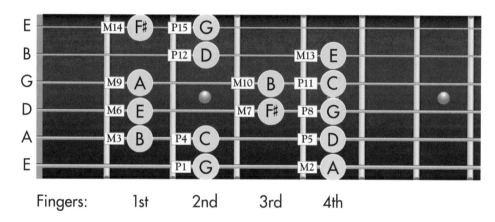

A little information on scales…

Intervals

- The number of the note as it appears linearly in a scale can be considered its **scale degree**
- The major scale has seven notes, or scale degrees, in it
- An **interval** is the distance (in step value) between two pitches

To define an interval, they are called unison, 2nd, 3rd, 4th, 5th, 6th, 7th, or 8th. The eighth note is the **octave**, and, although note degrees above the octave repeat themselves, the numbering can increase based on the distance from the **root** (original key note); for example, 9th, 10th, 11th, 12th, 13th, 14th, and 15th (two octaves higher than root, or **15ma**). Intervals that are beyond the range of an octave are called **compound intervals**.

Compound Intervals

- When a 2nd is an octave higher, it is called a 9th

- When a 3rd is an octave higher, it is called a 10th

- When a 4th is an octave higher, it is called an 11th

- When a 5th is an octave higher, it is called a 12th

- When a 6th is an octave higher, it is called a 13th

- When a 7th is an octave higher, it is called a 14th

- When an 8th is an octave higher, it is sometimes called a 15th

The names of intervals are distinguished by using these terms:

- Perfect (P)

- Major (M)

- Minor (m)

- Augmented (A)

- Diminished (d)

Every interval has a particular sound, flavor, and color based on the way the notes resonate together. Some intervals are referred to as **perfect** because of the way they resonate together. The ratio of their frequencies are simple whole numbers. You can sense their resonant wholeness if you listen to them carefully. Here are the main intervals and their qualities.

- The **perfect intervals** are:
  P1, P4, P5, and P8

- The **major intervals** are:
  M2, M3, M6, and M7

- If you lower a major interval by a half step, it becomes minor. The **minor intervals** are:
  m2, m3, m6, and m7

- If you lower a minor or perfect interval by a half step, it becomes diminished. The **diminished intervals** are:
  d2, d3, d4, d5, d6, and d7

- If you raise a major or perfect interval by a half step, it becomes augmented. The **augmented intervals** are:
  A2, A3, A4, A5, A6, and A7

A diminished or augmented 1st or 8th is theoretical, as is an augmented 7th. They technically exist but are never referred to because the 1st (root) or 8th (octave/root) of a scale is the center point that all other intervals revolve around within a scale or chord.

- Another symbol for diminished is a small circle next to a note or chord: C°

- Another symbol for augmented is a small plus sign next to a note or chord: C+

Here is a list of all intervals in relation to the 12-tone chromatic scale. They are linearly laid out in half-step intervals. An augmented 7th and augmented 1st are theoretical but are included here:

INTERVAL TABLE

Note	C	C#/Db	D	D#/Eb	E	F	F#/Gb	G	G#/Ab	A	A#/Bb	B
Chromatic Scale Degrees, 1/2-step increments		1	2	3	4	5	6	7	8	9	10	11
Major and Perfect Scale Intervals	P1		M2		M3	P4		P5		M6		M7
Minor Intervals		m2		m3					m6		m7	
Diminished Intervals	d2		d3		d4		d5	d6		d7		
Augmented Intervals	A7	A1		A2		A3	A4		A5		A6	

In regard to the previous diagram of the G major scale, it only represents one particular way to play the G major scale.

If you are interested in scale exercises, here are a few tips to help you get a visual of the major scale around the neck. I suggest singing every note you play.

1. Practice the previous major scale pattern, both forward and backward, starting from every fret on the low E string.

2. Practice the major scale in every position on the neck, up and down, but change the fingering so you start with your first finger.

3. Practice the major scale from the lowest note to its highest note on the neck, starting from every note on the guitar, up and down.

4. Make up your own.

SCALES (EXPERIENTIAL STUDY)

Listening

Now that you know the "academics" of the major scale, it's time to work on the emotional connection with it. As we progress, we will explore all sorts of scales. Understanding the academics of a scale *can* be important, but of much more *vital* importance is the tonal quality of the scale. That's the experiential aspect of the scale. As with everything else, this requires a meditative listening to the atmosphere that the tonality of a scale creates. Listen carefully to a major scale and experiment with soloing exclusively within it and feeling the quality of the tonality of it. In this scale, and all scales, find the notes that mean the most to you.

In the key of G major, a few chord progressions that you can perhaps record and jam over are listed below. Keep in mind that there are countless progressions that can be written with a major tonality. These are very simple.

G Major Chord Progressions

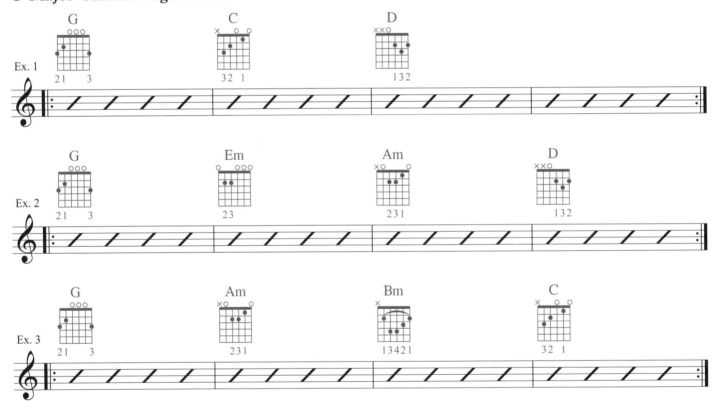

Write down a list of qualities you feel within the harmonic atmosphere of the major scale. Some ways it has been described are "uplifting," "happy," "bright," "cheerful," "sunshine," etc.

Memorizing the "color" of a scale is of much greater importance than understanding the academics of it, but they walk hand in hand, or finger in finger.

ADVANCED INTERVALS
(EXPERIENTIAL STUDY)

What we've covered so far in regard to scale degrees and intervals is all there really is to know about it. Of greater importance is being able to identify intervals just by hearing them and, of course, studying their personality. If you could identify an interval just by hearing it, you will find yourself *way* ahead of the game when it comes to improvising, writing music, communicating with other musicians, etc.

There are a host of very good apps you can look into that will help train your ear to memorize the sounds of intervals. Here are a few as of early 2018:

- My Ear Trainer
- Perfect Ear Trainer
- Complete Ear Trainer
- Functional Ear Trainer
- Chord Trainer Free

- Interval Ear Training
- Relative Pitch Free Interval Ear Training
- Ear Trainer Lite
- Complete Ear Trainer

And here are a few exercises you can do to help develop your connection with intervals:

1. Sit for a period and play the intervals listed below around the neck. As you do, listen very deeply to the quality of the interval. What does it sound like to you? What does it make you feel like? Etc. Then do this with all the other intervals, giving sufficient time to each all over the neck, in the following order:

   - Octaves
   - Perfect 5ths
   - Perfect 4ths
   - Major 3rds
   - Major 7ths

   - Major 6ths
   - Minor 7ths
   - Minor 3rds (Augmented 2nds)
   - Major 2nds

   - Augmented 4ths (Diminished 5ths)
   - Minor 6ths (Augmented 5ths)
   - Minor 2nds

2. Extend this to include compound intervals such as 9ths, 11ths, 13ths, etc.

3. Record 10 minutes of each interval at random places on the neck. It's important to use the lowest and highest registers of the guitar when doing this. Listen back carefully and meditate on the personality of each interval.

4. Record an hour of random intervals, using them all, from a minor 2nd to a 15th (double octave). Strike them once and let them ring out for 3–4 seconds, leaving a slight empty gap in the recording, followed by your voice naming the interval. When you listen back to this, try to name the interval in the gap. If you can name the actual note name when doing this, then congratulations, you have perfect pitch!

SCALES CONTINUED (ACADEMIC STUDY)

The Minor Scale

We've reviewed the major scale. Now we will review the **minor scale**. The minor scale, or its modal name, **Aeolian**, is a major scale with a lowered 3rd, 6th, and 7th. Perhaps a better way of putting it is: a minor scale is a major scale with a m3, m6, and m7 (or, ♭3rd, ♭6th, and ♭7th). Its scale degrees are as follows:

1, P2, m3, P4, P5, m6, m7, 8

or

1, 2, ♭3, 4, 5, ♭6, ♭7, 8

Here is the G minor scale in first position:

G MINOR SCALE

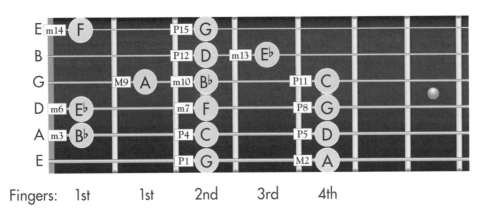

Apply all of the same academic and experiential practice techniques to the minor scale as are outlined for the major scale.

Here are some simple minor-key chord progressions to fool around with, record, and jam over:

G Minor Chord Progressions

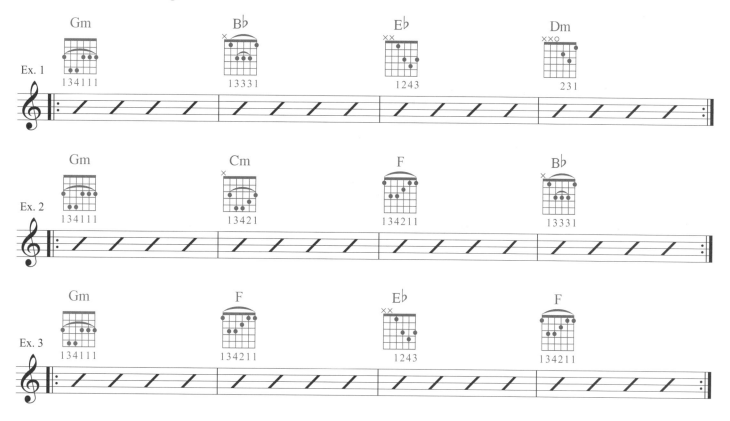

Pentatonic Scale

A **pentatonic scale** is a scale that contains only five notes within an octave (or more)—hence the name (penta = five, tonic = tone). There are, of course, a multitude of pentatonic scales you can create and play on the neck, but we will focus on the **major pentatonic scale**. The most conventional major pentatonic scale consists of the following scale degrees:

1, 2, 3, 5, 6

or

1, M2, M3, P5, M6

Here's an example of the major pentatonic scale in the key of G major. In this diagram, the second octave shows the scale degrees similarly to the first octave, instead of showing compound intervals. So, although the A on the D string can be considered a M9 when thinking of compound intervals (based on the root being on the third fret of the low E string), I've notated it as a M2. It's good to make the connection that a 2nd is also a 9th, and a 5th is also a 12th. The best time to use compound intervals is when spelling a chord (more on that later).

G MAJOR PENTATONIC SCALE

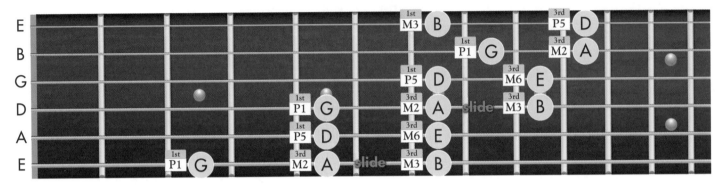

Fingers: Numbers in blue blocks on neck

Although this scale can be substituted for the G major scale, it does not contain all the "tension" notes. It could be considered more "country" or "rock" sounding than the full major scale.

As with the other scales, memorize the sound of this scale and enter its atmosphere. Major chord progressions, like the ones given in the previous sections, will work with this scale. This pentatonic scale is also useful for identifying more "real estate" on the neck in the key of G major. Try experimenting with soloing and using all the G major notes around the neck. Fool around with string bends, vibrato, trills, dynamics, etc.

Blues Scale

The blues scale is the motherload in rock and blues music. It's more of a custom-type scale in that there's no real rule as to what the blues scale is (at least not that I know of). The first blues scale I learned, which was within the first few weeks of playing the guitar, is the scale that my playing revolves around to this day in many chord-change situations. It's outlined below.

This scale is at the foundation of my finger awareness on the neck but takes a way-back seat to my ears. Meaning, I let my ears guide me when I'm improvising more than I let the academics of a scale guide me, but *both* can work together nicely.

Most blues scales are pentatonic-based, but this blues scale has some "tension" notes in it towards the upper end of the scale that can work. They are in pink. This blues scale, with the written tensions, can also be seen as a variation of the **Dorian mode**. I sometimes refer to this scale as the "Dorian blues." The Dorian mode is the second scale degree (mode) of the major scale, but more on that later.

Also, when considering scale degrees from a P1 to a P15 that cover the range of a two-octave scale, it's rare that certain intervals, such as a 3rd, would be called a 10th, or a 5th would be called a 12th, or a 7th called a 14th. So, in the scale illustration below, and in future ones that have fretboards, the most commonly used scale degrees are written in their lower interval number, and the only compound intervals that are written as the higher octave numbers are those that are usually used in chord voicings.

Intervals from root of scale:

P1, M2, M3, P4, P5, M6, M7, P8, M9, M10, P11, P12, M13, M14, P15

Commonly used scale degrees:

P1, M2, M3, P4, P5, M6, M7, P8, M9, M3, P11, P5, M13, M7, P1

G BLUES SCALE

Fingers: Numbers in blue blocks on neck

You may have noticed that the A on the high E string is indicated as a M9. Although this note could be considered the M17th from the G root on the low E string, it would only be theoretical to call it this. It would be more appropriately called the major 2nd (M2) or major 9th (M9).

As with the other scales, study these on both the academic and experiential levels.

If you watch virtually any rock guitar player, you will notice that they are usually maneuvering in this scale format. The moment I learned it, I felt as though a huge veil was lifted and an opening formed in my personal relationship with the neck and maneuvering around it.

Practicing Scales

I never practiced the blues scale; I just played around in it. There was a time when I was young and learning the guitar that I would practice every scale, every mode, in every key, up and down the neck, at various speeds, every day, among many other things. This was a purely academic, technique practice routine that I used to help develop my chops. There was some experiential value in it because I was focusing on the harmonic quality of the scales, but most of it was rote practicing.

These days, I might not recommend this kind of practice; it's terribly outdated. Instead, I would recommend understanding the academics of these scales and having them under your fingers (and the modes that we will be getting to), but instead of rote-type practicing, just play, play, play, play, play *music*… and not so much scales. Communicating with other musicians (no matter how good or bad you think you or they are), exploring your emotions in audio form, and constantly creating, exploring, and investigating in a connected way is all of much greater value in the long run than endlessly practicing scales up and down.

Try to always make what you're doing sound like music, even if you are just playing a scale. There is a different type of attention you will give to something you are playing when you are listening and expressing with your focus on making a musical statement, rather than by creating something that is pattern-based, finger-memory meandering.

In order for anything you play to sound like music, you have to hear it as a musical statement in your head. Then your fingers will slowly massage the note into what you are intending it to sound like, based on how you feel.

Exploring the Neck

While you are expanding your awareness of the neck in any particular key, what you are ultimately looking for is an organic, whole-neck awareness in any key. The best way to do this is to just experiment with notes that work in a key but are not necessarily within a particular scale pattern you may know. Doing this forces you to use your ear.

One thing that is helpful in the beginning is to connect scales that work together. For instance—and this was *big* for me when I was 13—if you are jamming out on, let's say "G blues," and you play the previous major pentatonic scale but starting a minor 3rd (three frets) higher than the root, G (which is Bb), the notes will work beautifully together. This will expand your awareness of that key on the neck.

The reason these two scales work together so well is because the key of Bb major is the **relative major** of G minor. Or, another way of saying it: G minor is the **relative minor** of Bb major (more on relative minor and major keys later).

Here is a diagram that shows the G blues scale and Bb major pentatonic scale in both the lower and upper octave. All of these notes are available to you. The big discovery for me at 13 was when I connected G blues, Bb major pentatonic, and the notes that are in between them that work but are not part of the scale pattern.

Experiment with connecting these scales with notes that work but are not part of the conventional scale patterns (i.e., G blues or Bb major pentatonic). In this diagram, I included some of the "tension" notes in certain positions and did not include scale degrees on the entire diagram.

G BLUES SCALE + Bb MAJOR PENTATONIC SCALE

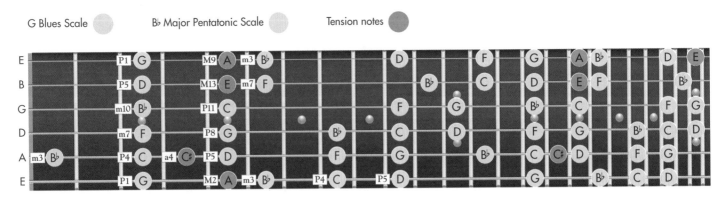

Whole-Neck Awareness in G Blues

The neck illustration below shows all the notes in G blues, or G Dorian blues. All the notes from the G Dorian blues are outlined in light yellow dots. All the notes from the relative Bb major pentatonic scale are in green dots, and all other notes that work on the neck but fall outside of the conventional fingering for G Dorian blues or Bb major pentatonic are in red. You may see the same tension notes in different colors; for instance, F on the first fret of the E strings in red, F on the sixth fret of the B string in light yellow, and F on the eighth fret of the A string in green. This is because some of the F notes are outlined in the blues scale, some in the major pentatonic scale, and some outside of the normal patterns for those scales.

The C♯ (or the augmented 4th/11th of the scale) is only represented in a few positions but can be sought out around the neck. But it's more of a "flavorful passing tone."

G BLUES SCALE + B♭ MAJOR PENTATONIC SCALE EXPANDED

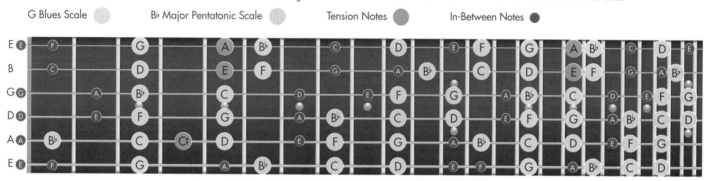

Try soloing over blues-type changes in the key of G and experiment with all the notes outside of the conventional scale patterns that work to your ear. At first, you may use your ears to connect familiar patterns, but eventually the patterns themselves take a back seat to your inner musical intention; in other words, you won't be thinking in terms of patterns or finger memory, but rather in a musical statement.

Make Every Note Work, Somehow

OK, so these are scales that seem to have parameters. That's fine, and you can work within them, but they are really just helpful maps. Try experimenting with notes that are outside of the key and see how they make you feel. These notes are sometimes called **passing tones**. You can use them to interconnect musical ideas. Also try experimenting with chromatics.

The thing that makes many of the outside notes work is the target note at the end of a phrase. You can create a line or melody that has some pretty obtuse notes in it, but, if you land on the right note at the end of a phrase, it has the uncanny ability to give an artistic distinction to the outside notes.

Experiment with playing phrases that have "wrong" notes in them, but **cadence** them to (end the phrase with) a strong target note such as the **tonic** (root, or 1 of the key) or a P5, P4, etc. I believe Miles Davis was one time quoted as saying, "You have to stay away from the butter notes."

The goal is to be completely present with the note, to become the note—meaning your attention is absorbed in it fully. There are infinite creative, intense, beautiful, quirky, powerfully nasty, tremendously enchanting, unique melodies within your inner being, and they are just waiting to come out. They want to come out through you. But you will not have access to them if you don't create an opening for them, and the only way to create an opening is to be completely present, still, relaxed, and open to allowing them when you are playing. You need to allow them to come out by trusting in the present moment of them. Geez, I know this must sound odd to some, but it's the best I can do!

KEY SIGNATURES AND THE CIRCLE OF 5THS

In music theory, the **circle of 5ths** is a sequence of pitches, or key tonalities, represented as a circle in which the next pitch is found seven semitones, or a 5th, higher than the last. Musicians and composers use the circle of 5ths to understand and describe the musical relationships among those pitches. The circle's design is helpful in composing and harmonizing melodies, building chords, and modulating to different keys within a composition.

The word **diatonic** basically means "within the scale you are working in." For instance, a C# is not diatonic to the key of C major, whereas B natural is.

The diatonic key signature is the indicator of the key that a particular composition is in. Each key has various sharps and flats that indicate that key. At the top of the circle of 5ths is the key of C major. This key has no sharps or flats. On a piano, it's all the white keys, starting from C.

If you progress to the right through the circle of 5ths, the next key is a perfect 5th away from the preceding one. So, in the key of C major, the 5th is G. A 5th away from G is the key of D, etc. Every time you move to the right to a new key, there is an additional sharp added to the key until you get to its enharmonic equivalent, which is where it turns into the flat keys. For instance, the key of B major has five sharps in it but is enharmonic to the key of C♭ major, which has seven flats in it, and so on.

The sharps, as they appear, are added a 5th away from each other, so…

SHARP KEYS		
Key of	**Number of Sharps**	**What They Are**
C	0	
G	1	F#
D	2	F#, C#
A	3	F#, C#, G#
E	4	F#, C#, G#, D#
B	5	F#, C#, G#, D#, A#
F#	6	F#, C#, G#, D#, A#, E#
C#	7	F#, C#, G#, D#, A#, E#, B#

Conversely, if you follow the circle of 5ths to the left, it progresses in 4ths and the flats appear a 4th away from each other.

FLAT KEYS		
Key of	**Number of Flats**	**What They Are**
F	1	B♭
B♭	2	B♭, E♭
E♭	3	B♭, E♭, A♭
A♭	4	B♭, E♭, A♭, D♭
D♭	5	B♭, E♭, A♭, D♭, G♭
G♭	6	B♭, E♭, A♭, D♭, G♭, C♭
C♭	7	B♭, E♭, A♭, D♭, G♭, C♭, F♭

Relative Major and Minor Keys

Relative minor keys were briefly mentioned earlier when discussing the major scale. Relative minor and relative major are two scales that share the same notes and same key signature but have different tonics and tonalities. The root of a relative minor scale is a major 6th above the root of its corresponding relative major scale. And the root of a relative major scale is a minor 3rd higher than the root of its relative minor scale. So, for instance, E minor is the relative minor scale of G major, and G major is the relative major scale of E minor. They both have the same notes in them but have different roots. This is outlined nicely in the circle of 5ths.

The circle of 5ths can give you an instant visual of related elements, such as:

- The sharps or flats in a key
- What those sharps or flats are
- The relative minor and major keys

In this diagram of the circle of 5ths, the outside keys are the major keys, the inside minor keys are the corresponding relative minor keys, and the notation on the inside shows the sharps and flats of the various keys as they appear on the staff.

CIRCLE OF 5THS

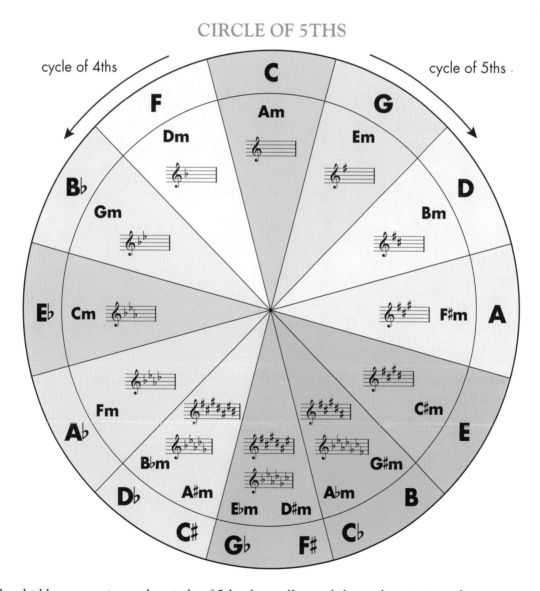

There are other hidden mysteries to the circle of 5ths that will reveal themselves in time if you continue to use it. I recommend memorizing the entire circle of 5ths and knowing it cold, without having to count or think. This can be helpful in many situations.

NOTES ON MANUSCRIPT (ACADEMIC STUDY)

You may or may not be interested in knowing how to read or write music, but it's perhaps a good idea to at least understand the basic mapping of written notes. This is sometimes intimidating to people, but really, with a little focused attention, it's quite easy and practical.

Staff

In most contemporary music cultures, the **staff** (or **staves**, plural) is a set of five horizontal lines and four spaces that each represent a different musical pitch. Below is a typical five-line musical staff.

G-Clef

The staff doesn't mean anything until it has a clef. The **clef** is the first symbol on the left side of a staff that indicates what the actual notes are on the staff. The most common clef is the **treble clef**, also called the **G-clef** (because it "circles" a G on the staff).

The G-clef has an odd way of always getting me excited when I see it. Not sure what that is, but whenever I even look at one, it seems to represent an ancient peace and comfort. Eh… go figure.

The treble clef in the example below indicates that the note that is written is C. It lives on the ledger line right below the staff. **Ledger lines** are short lines written above or below the staff for notes pitched outside the staff. This particular C is also known as **middle C** and is basically the middle of the piano. It's also conventionally known as "C4." Some programmers of samplers call middle C, "C3." And most pieces of Yamaha gear refer to middle C as C3. It's not conventional to call it C3; it's traditionally known as C4.

Bass Clef

The next most common clef is the **bass clef**, or **F-clef** (because the "dot" at the head of the clef is on an F, and the two dots surround the F).

Perhaps it's not as sexy as the G-clef, but the notes that accompany it are lower.

Here's the bass clef with middle C:

Grand Staff

When you put the treble clef and the bass clef together (but on separate staves), you create a **grand staff**. This is what keyboard players, harp players, and some other instruments use.

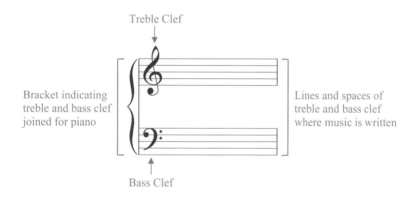

CLEFS (ADVANCED)

There are other clefs that are used by various transposing instruments at times. These clefs indicate middle C appearing at different places on the staff. The reason for them is basically so the people writing and reading music do not have to write excessive ledger lines to fit the range of a particular instrument. Unless you decide to study composition and compose, it's unlikely you will ever use these other clefs. All the notes written below are actually the same exact note, middle C.

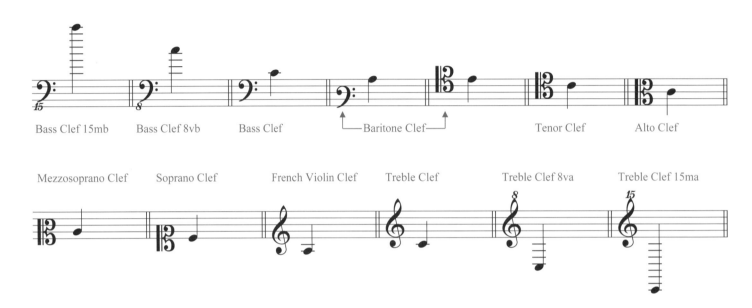

Percussion Clef

One other clef and staff worth pointing out is used for non-pitched percussion instruments. The **percussion staff** does not indicate notes—usually because most percussion instruments do not produce conventional tones. The staves for non-pitched percussion instruments can vary from not having any lines to up to five lines, depending on the instruments reading for it. Mallet percussion instruments—xylophone, vibes, marimba, etc.—use pitched clefs and normal staves.

The percussion clef is two vertical slashes:

Below are some non-pitched percussion staves using one-, two-, three-, four-, and five-line staves.

Various Percussion Staves

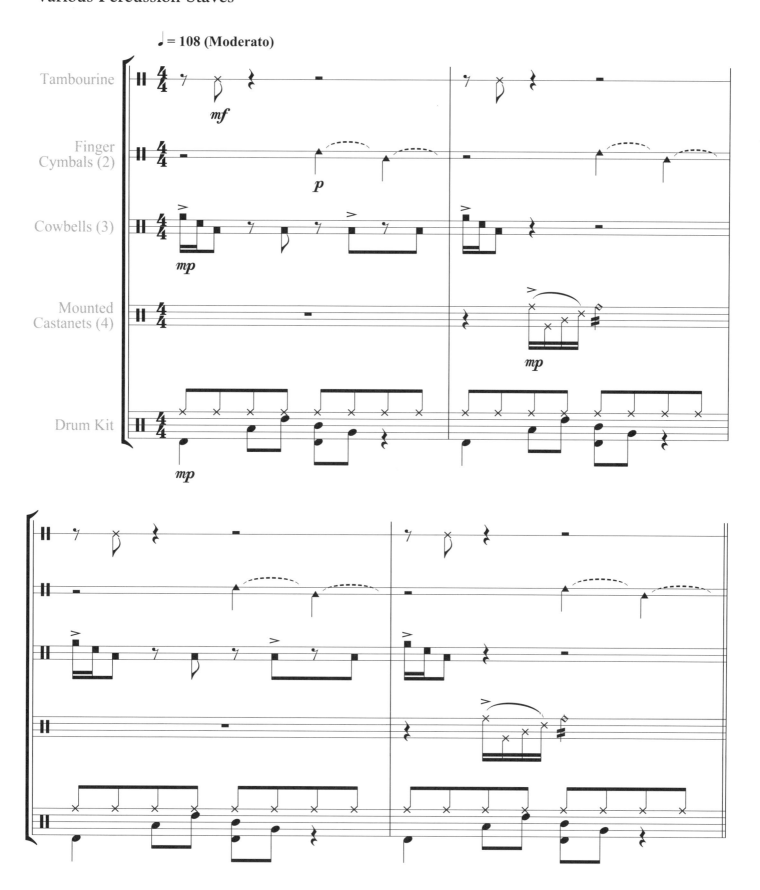

TRANSPOSING INSTRUMENTS

Guitar Transposition

The guitar is a **transposing instrument**. What that basically means is, whenever you read music on the guitar, the note that actually comes out of the guitar sounds an octave lower than where it is being read in the music. So, if you were to read middle C on the guitar, you would play the eighth fret on the low E string or the third fret on the A string (they are the same note). However, the note that sounds is an octave lower than middle C. To actually hear middle C on the guitar, you would have to play the note an octave higher than where it's written, such as on the first fret of the B string (or the fifth fret of the G string, or the 10th fret of the D string). Yup, that can be confusing. But just keep in mind that guitar music is written an octave higher than where it is sounding; that is, guitar music, when played on the guitar, sounds an octave lower than where it's written. If it wasn't this way, and the guitar was a non-transposing instrument, a guitar player would have to read and write music in both bass and treble clef. Thank goodness for transposing instruments!

The same holds true for the electric bass and contra bass (or double bass) in the orchestra.

Many other instruments are transposing instruments, but not all by an octave. Some are two octaves, a perfect 5th, a 9th, a 2nd, etc.

In classical music, musicians that play transposing instruments need to receive their parts already transposed. It's been a longstanding practice that, when composers write their scores, they write "transposed scores," which basically means that any instruments that are transposing instruments are *written* transposed in the score. In the beginning of the 20th century, some composers started to write their scores in **concert pitch**, meaning that all notes in the written score sound the actual notes that are written. All my scores are concert-pitch scores, with the exception of instruments that are an octave or double-octave transposition (xylophone sounds *15ma*). It just seems to make much more sense to me to write concert scores.

Here is a list of a host of instruments and their transposition:

NON-TRANSPOSING INSTRUMENTS		
Instrument	Interval of Transposition	Clef(s)
Violin	Concert Pitch	Treble
Viola	Concert Pitch	Alto/Treble
Cello	Concert Pitch	Bass
Harp	Concert Pitch	Grand Staff
Flute	Concert Pitch	Treble
Oboe	Concert Pitch	Treble
Bassoon	Concert Pitch	Bass
Trombone	Concert Pitch	Bass
Bass Trombone	Concert Pitch	Bass/Tenor
Tuba	Concert Pitch	Bass
Marimba	Concert Pitch	Treble
Vibraphone	Concert Pitch	Treble
Timpani	Concert Pitch	Bass
Piano	Concert Pitch	Grand Staff
Organ	Concert Pitch	Grand Staff
Harpsichord	Concert Pitch	Grand Staff

TRANSPOSING INSTRUMENTS		
Instrument	Interval of Transposition	Clef(s)
Double Bass	Sounds one **octave** *lower* than written	Bass
Guitar	Sounds one **octave** *lower* than written	Treble
Piccolo	Sounds one **octave** *higher* than written	Treble
Alto Flute	Sounds one **perfect 4th** *lower* than written	Treble
English Horn	Sounds one **perfect 5th** *lower* than written	Treble
Clarinet in B♭	Sounds one **Major 2nd** *lower* than written	Treble
Clarinet in A	Sounds one **minor 3rd** *lower* than written	Treble
Clarinet in E♭	Sounds one **Major 6th** *lower* than written	Treble
Bass Clarinet in B♭	Sounds one **Major 9th** *lower* than written	Bass
Contrabassoon	Sounds one **octave** *lower* than written	Bass
Soprano Sax in B♭	Sounds one **Major 2nd** *lower* than written	Treble
Alto Sax in E♭	Sounds one **Major 6th** *lower* than written	Treble
Tenor Sax in B♭	Sounds one **Major 9th** *lower* than written	Treble
Baritone Sax in E♭	Sounds one **octave** + one **Major 6th** *lower* than written	Treble
French Horn	Sounds one **Perfect 5th** *lower* than written	Treble
Trumpet in B♭	Sounds one **Major 2nd** *lower* than written	Treble
Glockenspiel	Sounds two **octaves** *higher* than written	Treble
Xylophone	Sounds one **octave** *higher* than written	Treble
Celesta	Sounds one **octave** *higher* than written	Grand Staff

MUSICAL NOTES

Below is an outline of the musical notes on the grand staff and how they relate to the piano (pianos usually have notes that go above and below the indicated notes). When a note is written above or below the staff, it is written on ledger lines.

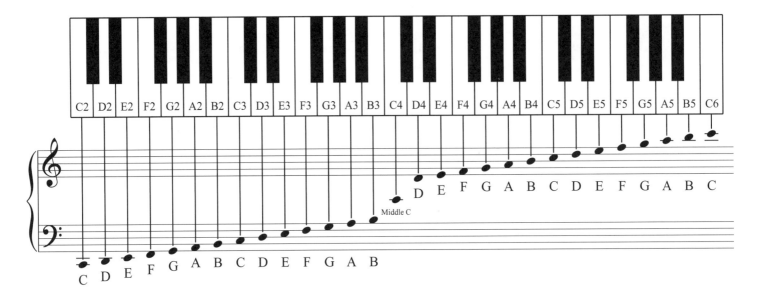

I have always felt it was a good idea for anyone who's serious about making music their career to memorize the notes on the staff without using mnemonic devices such as "Every Good Boy Does Fine," which helps to memorize the notes on the lines of the treble clef staff.

This can create a crutch. I suggest just memorizing all the notes. And here's a good way to do it, while training your ear at the same time:

1. Get some manuscript paper and write five pages of noteheads from C4 to C5. Then read back their names.

2. Do the same, but this time with C5 to C6, then C6 to C7, then C7 to C8. If you plan on reading guitar music in the highest registers, knowing the ledger lines above the staff is very useful.

3. Do the same with these notes below the treble clef. Since the guitar includes notes on these low ledger lines, it's good to know them immediately by sight.

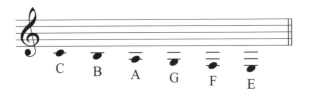

4. Do the same with the notes from C3 to C4, then C2 to C3, and even C1 to C2 if you are into it.

5. Now write random notes with various sharps, flats, or naturals from C1 to C8 and read it back, naming each note you see.

If you've boned up on your interval ear training, then try writing five pages of completely atonal music that spans the entire grand staff. Then, while reading them back, sing every note you wrote while naming it.

If you can do this accurately, I will kiss your ass in Starbucks' window!

CHORDS (ACADEMIC STUDY)

Much can be said about chords, but let's start with the academics.

- Two or more pitches played together is a **chord**

- Two-note chords are called **double stops**

- Three-note chords are called **triads**

- Chords greater than three notes are called **extended chords**

When writing guitar chords in diagram form (sometimes called **tablature**, or "tab"), I prefer to write them as follows, but I use the abbreviated versions more often:

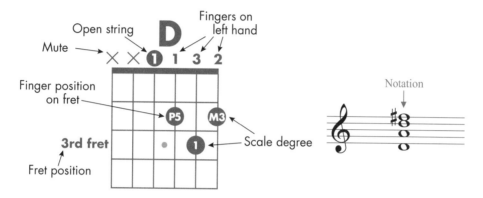

Perhaps there's more information in the way it's written above than necessary, but I just like doing it this way because it explains everything and, when you start writing your own chords, which may be more complex than conventional chords, it might be nice to include all of the above information. Of course, you can simplify this, and in your guitar travels you will see various ways that people notate chord tab. Most common is to show the fingering numbers on the actual notes on the neck or at the nut. Here are variations of the same message:

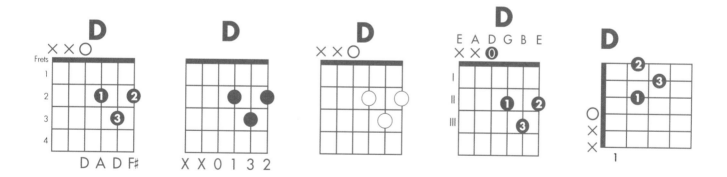

Before we discuss chord scales and how various chords work within a scale, it may be a good idea to first learn a whole bunch of chords, get them under your fingers, and start strumming away on them.

Learn and memorize every open chord on the guitar, and then from there, venture into barre chords and chords that have odder fingerings and tension notes.

There is a plethora of good books that you can purchase that include tons and tons of chords in tab form. Try searching online for "open chords on guitar," or anything like that, and you will find many standard chords for the guitar.

CHORDS (EXPERIENTIAL STUDY)

In the previous chord diagram for a D chord, there was a lot of academic information about the chord, but you will never really know a D chord until you play it and listen to it carefully.

Every chord has a story to it, a personality, color, psychological weight, vibe, etc. Whenever you learn a new chord, be it a simple open chord or a complex "jazz" chord, it's vital to meditate on the experiential aspect of the chord. Try to live inside the emotional atmosphere of the chord. I guess what I mean is, become the chord by giving it your full listening attention and bathe in its eminence. You need to be very still mentally to do this.

Ask yourself how this chord makes you feel. What does it remind you of? What color or emotion would you associate with this chord? What is the story of the chord? Also memorize the name of the chord based on its sound instead of just memorizing its finger positions and scale. You will develop a personal relationship with the chord.

There are a few great exercises you can do that I used to do with Joe Satriani when I took lessons from him between the ages of 12 and 15.

Grab a friend that plays guitar and sit across from each other in a dimly lit room. Have one person play any chord by strumming it once and then lightly picking out all the notes. Have the other person listen intensely to the chord and make up a story about what that chord sounds like to him/her. This could be anything—colors, words, etc.—but describing a mental scene will build your personal relationship with that chord. Then try to name the chord. The trick is always in listening to it deeply, in presence.

This really worked wonders for me as a youngster, and I still do it.

Another exercise is to do the same example as above but by yourself. Record an hour or so of random chords, playing each for 20 seconds and then naming the chord at the end. When you listen back, try investing yourself in each chord completely and then naming it before the recording of your voice names the chord.

Start your own chord library by building chords that your fingers find a place for as they are guided by your ears. This will increase your chord vocabulary. Some of the first "flavor" chords I entered into my chord dictionary as a youngster are below (there are tons, but I included just a few).

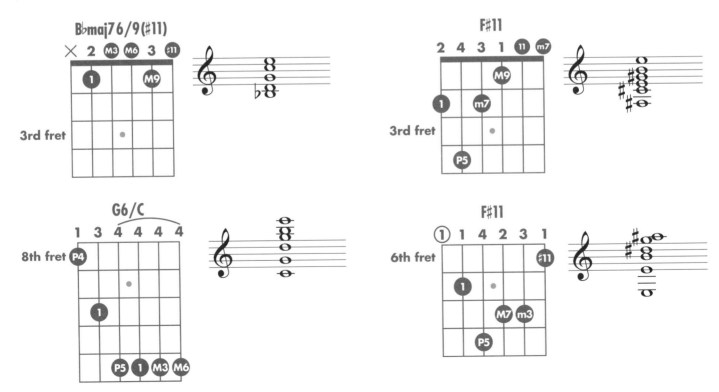

CHORD SPELLING
(ACADEMIC STUDY)

It can seem confusing when it comes time to name a chord. Chords get their names from the scale degrees (relative to the root) that are contained within the chord. Some identical chords can have various names that sort of mean the same thing. The symbols and names that you will see can vary. In this chapter's list, I've used the chord formulas and names that have always made sense to me, but you may see them written differently at times. Sometimes they will be written wrong, and sometimes it's just another way of naming two identical chords.

Chord Spelling Library

There can be a lot of confusion when it comes to what the "rules" are when naming a chord. Some are obvious, and some are questionable. But the rules of thumb are:

- If a chord has a "major" in its name, it must contain a major 3rd

- If it has a "minor" in its name, then it must contain a minor 3rd

- If there's a 7th in a minor chord, it will be a m7, unless otherwise described in the chord name, such as a Cm(maj7)

Once you start understanding the basic formula and the practicality of the way chords are written, certain things about the naming of a chord and its voicings will make sense. But, at times, songwriters can be referring to different chords than what they've written down because they learned to write them a particular way that doesn't necessarily jive with a chord's appropriate name. If you are particular about the chord you want, it's a good idea to provide the tab for the chord, or the actual notes.

A few more "relative" rules of thumb are:

- A "sus" chord usually refers to a **suspended** 4th but can also refer to a suspended 2nd at times. It's best to be specific. When "sus" is applied to a chord, it is conventionally indicating that the 3rd of the chord is being replaced by either the 2nd or the 4th. So, there are no 3rds in sus chords.

- Although a "2" is the same scale degree as the 9th, the 9th is an octave higher than the 2nd, or an octave and major 2nd higher than the root. But you might see something like "G2" even though the actual 2nd in the chord is a 9th away from the root. A better way to write that chord with the 9th might be "G(sus9)." The notes in that chord would contain the scale degrees 1, 5, and 9, but that's a relatively unconventional way of referring to the chord.

- A ♭7th in a chord can indicate a **minor seventh** or a **dominant seventh** chord. Its use as a minor 7th requires that the chord includes a minor 3rd, as well. When a 7th is referred to as a dominant 7th, it usually means that there is a major 3rd in the chord.

- A **tritone** is the interval of an augmented 4th or diminished 5th (same thing). This is the interval that gives a dominant seventh chord its flavor.

- The voicing progression of major chords as you add tensions to the chord, up to the 13th, might theoretically look like this: 1–3–5–7–9–11–13. But it's very common to not include a 3rd in a chord if it has an 11th because of the ♭9th interval that is created between the 3rd and 11th. It's very dissonant. And it's common for a 13th chord to not have a 5th, 9th, or 11th—you may see it all sorts of ways. Most of the time, the chords that are surrounding it will help tell you what the other scale degrees can be.

- If the name of a chord has parentheses in it, it usually means that those scale degrees are added to the chord and do not necessarily have an effect on the description of the chord outside of the parentheses. For instance, a C13 chord implies that the chord perhaps has a 1, 3, 5, ♭7, 9, 11, and 13, but the 3rd and 5th can be omitted. However, a chord that is spelled C(add13) or C(13) means the 13th is added to the chord but does not dictate any other notes in the chord. So, the scale tones of a C(add13) would be 1–3–5–13. Any time you see scale degrees in parentheses, they are referring to those scale degrees being added to the chord.

- An **upper-structure chord** usually refers to a chord that sits on top of a bass note, such as Emaj7/C.

- An **upper-structure triad** usually refers to a triad that is built on top of a bass note, such as G/C or C/G.

- A **hybrid-structure chord**, or **poly chord**, is a chord on top of another chord, such as Bsus/Faug.

- A **tripto-poly chord** (I may have made that up) is three chords stacked on top of each other.

- A **quadra-poly chord**, or **double-poly chord**, is four chords stacked on top of each other.

- You may discover various ways to name a chord that makes sense. Don't let it confuse you. Naming chords can seem ambiguous, but understanding the basic principles and nomenclature of chord spellings will help you to write a chord symbol for your chord that gets the point across and is not written wrong.

- You can add any scale degree to a chord that works for you. If it's not any kind of a 1, 3, or 5, it's called a **tension**. Tension notes could be considered any kind of 7th, 9th, 11th, 13th, or minor, augmented, or diminished scale degree.

- When adding tensions to a chord, those tensions would usually reflect the key of the progression, or they would make some kind of harmonic sense based on the chords surrounding it. For example, if you were in the key of C major and playing a conventional C major chord progression, chances are, you would not be putting a ♭9th on a C major chord. But you certainly can.

If you are playing freeform chords that are not necessarily based on a particular chord scale or progression, then you can basically add any scale degree that sounds good to you. An example would be if you were given just a C major chord to solo over. You can obviously play the C major scale, but since a C major chord contains the 1, 3, and 5 of the major scale, you can technically play any note that does not conflict with the 1, 3, or 5. Technically, you can play any note you want, but to make conventional melodic sense, this rule of thumb applies. For instance, you can play the following scales (and more):

$$1 - ♭2 - 3 - ♯4 - 5 - ♭6 - 7$$
$$1 - ♯2 - 3 - 4 - 5 - ♯6 - 7$$
$$1 - 2 - 3 - 4 - 5 - ♭6 - 7$$
$$1 - ♭2 - 3 - ♯4 - 5 - 6 - ♭7$$

Try experimenting with these scales over a C major chord to hear the different tonalities they create. Also, try writing down all the scales that can "work" over a C major chord.

But, if the chord *is* based on a particular key or chord-scale progression, or if you start venturing into the same odd notes written in the scales above, it could sound pretty bad.

A chord that has the scale degrees 1, ♭3, ♭5, and ♭7 is called a **min7♭5** chord, or a **half-diminished** chord. The chord symbol for half diminished is ⁱ (C⁰7, or Cm7♭5).

The term **voicing**, when applied to a chord, refers to the order of the scale degrees in the chord, from low to high.

According to conventional definition, an **altered chord** is a chord with any non-diatonic pitch. But usually, altered refers to the augmenting or diminishing of the 2nd and/or 5th of the scale or chord.

Below is a Chord Symbol Dictionary that outlines a chord's symbol, chord type, chord scale tones, alternate names for the chord, and comments from me about the chord. I used "C" as the root, but obviously, the root can be anything—the suffix that defines the chord would not change.

The "chord type" column shows a written version of its name with perhaps a little more clarity to it. There are also alternative names given for most chords. The main chord symbols are usually the ones I use because they are the clearest.

The "chord scale degrees" column shows which chord scale degrees are represented in the name of the chord. You will undoubtedly find some ambiguity in the various ways people write and name dense chords because there are various understandings of what some could mean. But the most important thing about a chord, as mentioned, is not the theory that it's based on or the academic knowledge of what it is; the main point is the sound, flavor, and atmosphere the chord creates with its emotional colors.

CHORD SYMBOL DICTIONARY

Chord Symbol	Chord Type	Chord Scale Degrees	Alternate Name (*Try to avoid using these*)	Comments
C5	Power Chord	1–5	N/A	A "5" chord indicates that the chord only consists of the 1st and 5th scale degrees.
C	Major Triad	1–3–5	CM, C^	A major triad has the 1st, major 3rd, and the 5th of the major scale in it. A triangle represents a triad.
Cmaj7	Major Seven	1–3–5–7	CMaj7, CM7, CMa7, Cma7, C^7	A major 7th chord has a major 3rd and a major 7th in it. The 5th can be omitted.
Cmaj9	Major Nine	1–3–5–7–9	CMaj9, CM9, CMa9, Cma9, C^9	A major 9th chord usually has a major 3rd, major 7th, and 9th. The 5th can be omitted.
Cmaj11	Major Eleven	1–3–5–7–9–11	CMaj11, CM11, Cma11, CMa11, C^11	Because of dissonance, the major 3rd is usually omitted in an 11th chord. The 5th can be omitted, too.
Cmaj13	Major Thirteen	1–3–5–7–9–11–13	CMaj13, CM13, Cma13, CMa13, C^13	Most commonly, a major 13th chord includes the 1st, major 3rd, major 7th, and 13th. The 5th, 9th, and 11th can be in the chord, but usually not the 3rd if there is an 11th. In cases like these chords, it's always best to write them out in tab or notation if you want to be specific.
C6	Major Six	1–3–5–6	C(add6)	When a chord symbol has parentheses around a scale degree, it means the note is added to the chord without any other special alteration.

CHORD SYMBOL DICTIONARY

Chord Symbol	Chord Type	Chord Scale Degrees	Alternate Name (*Try to avoid using these*)	Comments
C2	Two Chord	1–2–5	C(sus2), C(sus9)	Sometimes referred to as just a "2" chord. In a sus2 chord, the 2nd takes the place of the 3rd. The 2nd is suspended. A 9th is usually used in place of the 2nd.
Csus	Suspended 4th	1–4–5	C(sus4), Csus4	This is sometimes called the "amen" chord. The 4th is suspended (it takes the place of the 3rd) and has a pull to resolve to the 3rd.
C(add9)	Add Nine	1–3–5–9	Cadd9, C(9)	An add9 chord retains the major 3rd and has no kind of 7th.
C6/9	Six-Nine	1–3–5–6–9	C(6/9), Cadd6/9, C(6add9)	Sometimes the 5th is left out of this chord, and occasionally the 3rd.
Cmaj7♭5	Major Seven Flat-Five	1–3–♭5–7	CM7(♭5), Cmaj7(♭5)	It's important to note that, although a ♯4th and a ♭5th are enharmonic, many people call the ♭5 a ♯4th or ♯11, but it would be incorrect to do so if the chord was based on a scale with a perfect 4th in it.
Cmaj7♯5	Major Seven Sharp-Five	1–3–♯5–7	CM7(♯5), Cmaj7(♯5)	The same holds true here. If the chord is based on a scale that has a ♭6 and a perfect 5th in it, you would call the ♯5 a ♭6 (or ♭13) instead. Cmaj7♯5 implies there is usually a natural 6th in the tonality of the scale.
Cmaj7(♯11)	Major Seven Add Sharp-Eleven	1–3–5–7–♯11	CM7(♯11), Cma7(add♯11)	You can also voice a chord like this with a ♯4th instead of a ♯11th. If this is the case, you would still call the tension note a ♯11th, and not a ♯4th. Although calling it a ♯4th would make more sense, it's not common.
Cmaj7(6/9♯11)	Major Seven Add Six, Nine, and Sharp-Eleven	1–3–5–6–7–9–♯11	Cmaj13(♯11), C Lydian	This chord pretty much outlines the Lydian tonality. It has all the scale degrees in it. ♯11th chords work well with a major 3rd in them.
Cm	Minor Triad	1–♭3–5	Cmin, C-	If a chord is called "minor," then it must have a minor 3rd in it.

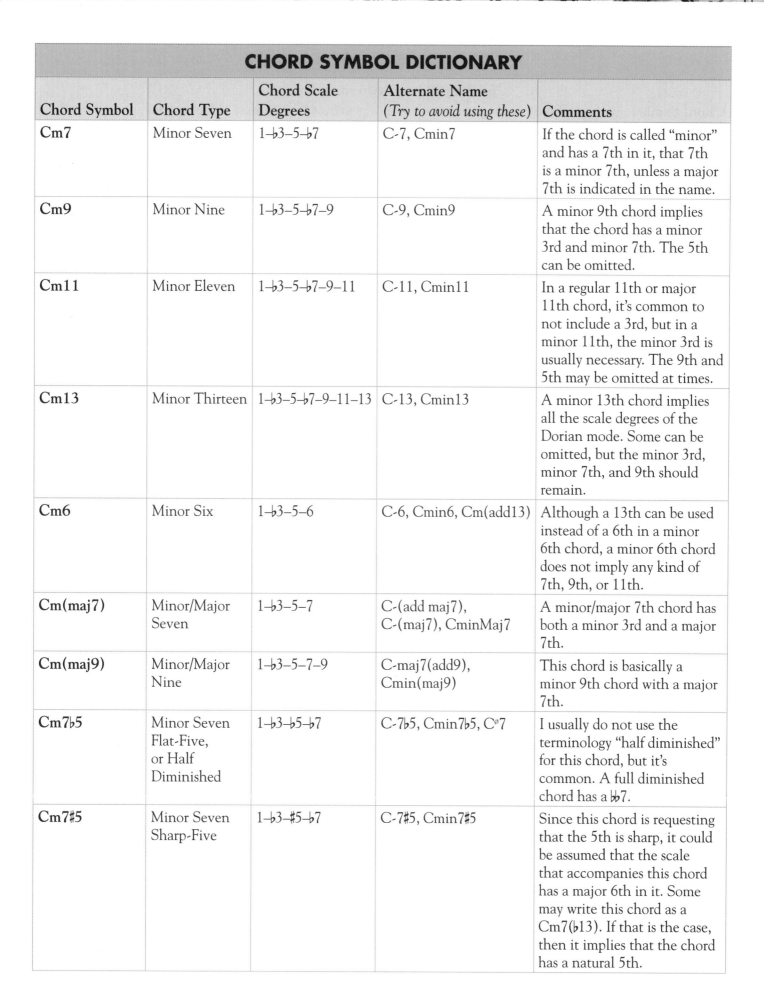

CHORD SYMBOL DICTIONARY

Chord Symbol	Chord Type	Chord Scale Degrees	Alternate Name (*Try to avoid using these*)	Comments
Cm7	Minor Seven	1–♭3–5–♭7	C-7, Cmin7	If the chord is called "minor" and has a 7th in it, that 7th is a minor 7th, unless a major 7th is indicated in the name.
Cm9	Minor Nine	1–♭3–5–♭7–9	C-9, Cmin9	A minor 9th chord implies that the chord has a minor 3rd and minor 7th. The 5th can be omitted.
Cm11	Minor Eleven	1–♭3–5–♭7–9–11	C-11, Cmin11	In a regular 11th or major 11th chord, it's common to not include a 3rd, but in a minor 11th, the minor 3rd is usually necessary. The 9th and 5th may be omitted at times.
Cm13	Minor Thirteen	1–♭3–5–♭7–9–11–13	C-13, Cmin13	A minor 13th chord implies all the scale degrees of the Dorian mode. Some can be omitted, but the minor 3rd, minor 7th, and 9th should remain.
Cm6	Minor Six	1–♭3–5–6	C-6, Cmin6, Cm(add13)	Although a 13th can be used instead of a 6th in a minor 6th chord, a minor 6th chord does not imply any kind of 7th, 9th, or 11th.
Cm(maj7)	Minor/Major Seven	1–♭3–5–7	C-(add maj7), C-(maj7), CminMaj7	A minor/major 7th chord has both a minor 3rd and a major 7th.
Cm(maj9)	Minor/Major Nine	1–♭3–5–7–9	C-maj7(add9), Cmin(maj9)	This chord is basically a minor 9th chord with a major 7th.
Cm7♭5	Minor Seven Flat-Five, or Half Diminished	1–♭3–♭5–♭7	C-7♭5, Cmin7♭5, Cø7	I usually do not use the terminology "half diminished" for this chord, but it's common. A full diminished chord has a ♭♭7.
Cm7♯5	Minor Seven Sharp-Five	1–♭3–♯5–♭7	C-7♯5, Cmin7♯5	Since this chord is requesting that the 5th is sharp, it could be assumed that the scale that accompanies this chord has a major 6th in it. Some may write this chord as a Cm7(♭13). If that is the case, then it implies that the chord has a natural 5th.

CHORD SYMBOL DICTIONARY

Chord Symbol	Chord Type	Chord Scale Degrees	Alternate Name (*Try to avoid using these*)	Comments
C7	Dominant Seven	1–3–5–♭7	Cdom7	A chord that has a "7" in its name, but does not have a major or minor label, implies a minor 7th and a major 3rd are in the chord.
C9	Dominant Nine	1–3–5–♭7–9	C7(add9), Cdom9	The reason you would not write this as a C(add9) is because that would imply there is no kind of 7th in the chord. A C9 implies a major 3rd and minor 7th are present in the chord.
C11	Dominant Eleven	1–3–5–♭7–9–11	C9(sus)	The spelling of the scale degrees is a bit of an anomaly for an 11th chord. An 11th chord implies a major 3rd, but most often there is no 3rd, though it must have a minor 7th. The 9th and 5th are sometimes omitted, but if that's the case, it's best to call the chord something else, such as C7(sus).
C13	Dominant Thirteen	1–3–5–♭7–9–11–13	C13(sus)	This chord implies all the notes of the Mixolydian scale, but if there is an 11th in the chord, the 3rd is usually omitted. Most 13th chords have a major 3rd and minor 7th, and the 11th is omitted.
C7sus	Dominant Seven Suspended 4th	1–4–5–♭7	C11	Sometimes written as an 11th chord but without the 3rd or 9th.
C7♭5	Dominant Seven Flat-Five	1–3–♭5–♭7	N/A	This is self-explanatory.
C7♯5	Dominant Seven Sharp-Five	1–3–♯5–♭7	N/A	This is self-explanatory.
C7♭9	Dominant Seven Flat-Nine	1–3–5–♭7–♭9	C7(add♭9), C7(♭9), C7alt9	An altered scale: 1, m2, A2, M3, d5, A5, and m7 (1, ♭2, ♯2, 3, ♭5, ♯5, and ♭7). This is why the suffix "alt" may be used sometimes. It's best to write the scale degree you want in the name.

CHORD SYMBOL DICTIONARY

Chord Symbol	Chord Type	Chord Scale Degrees	Alternate Name (*Try to avoid using these*)	Comments
C7♯9	Dominant Seven Sharp-Nine	1–3–5–♭7–♯9	C7(add♯9), C7alt9	Similar to the C7♭9 chord, this chord works with an altered scale. Although you may see this chord written with "alt" in the name, it's best not to use that label unless you are specifying that the scale to use is an altered scale.
C7♭5(♭9)	Dominant Seven Flat-Five Add Flat-Nine	1–3–♭5–♭7–♭9	C7alt, Calt, C7(♭5,♭9), C7♭5(add♭9)	The way it's written is the best way to write it. The altered scale is usually referred to in a chord like this.
C7♯5(♭9)	Dominant Seven Sharp-Five Add Flat-Nine	1–3–♯5–♭7–♭9	Calt, C7alt, C7(♯5/♭9), C7♯5(add♭9)	The way it's written is the best way to write it. The altered scale is usually referred to in a chord like this.
C9♭5	Dominant Nine Flat-Five	1–3–♭5–♭7–9	C9(♭5)	Because it's a 9th chord, it needs to have a major 3rd, minor 7th, and a 9th, but in this case, it also needs to have a ♭5, or d5.
C9♯5	Dominant Nine Sharp-Five	1–3–♯5–♭7–9	C9(+5), C9(♯5), C9(alt5), C9(aug5)	Because it's a 9th chord, it needs to have a major 3rd, minor 7th, and a 9th, but in this case, it also needs to have a ♯5, or aug5.
C13(♯11)	Dominant Thirteen Sharp-Eleven	1–3–5–♭7–9–♯11–13	C13(add♯11)	Another chord that has all the notes in the scale. Since the 11th is sharp, having a 3rd in the chord is appropriate. This is a cool chord!
C13(♭9)	Dominant Thirteen Flat-Nine	1–3–5–♭7–♭9–11–13	C13(add♭9)	In a chord like this, although an 11th may be implied, it is usually left out if there is a major 3rd in the chord.
C11(♭9)	Dominant Eleven Flat-Nine	1–3–5–♭7–♭9–11	C11(add♭9)	Since this is an 11th chord, it implies a major 3rd that is rarely used. With a ♭9 in the chord, playing a major 3rd would be very unlikely if you saw this chord symbol. It would be very dissonant, as the chord would have a minor 9th, major 3rd, and perfect 4th (or 11th). But then again, some people like that.

CHORD SYMBOL DICTIONARY

Chord Symbol	Chord Type	Chord Scale Degrees	Alternate Name (*Try to avoid using these*)	Comments
Caug	Augmented Triad	1–3–♯5	C+	An augmented triad is a chord that has two major 3rd intervals in it. The augmented scale is a "hexatonic" scale, meaning it only has six notes in it: 1–♯2–3–5–♭6–7.
Caug7	Dominant Seven Augmented	1–3–♯5–♭7	C7aug, C+7	Since it's a 7th chord, it must have a major 3rd and a minor 7th in it, but the augmented title tells you the 5th is sharp.
C°	Diminished Triad	1–♭3–♭5	Cdim	This is a minor triad with a ♭5. This chord is based on the diminished scale, which is an eight-note (octatonic) scale built by alternating whole and half steps from any root note.
C°7	Diminished Seven	1–♭3–♭5–♭♭7	Cdim7	A diminished 7th is a diminished triad with a 7th that's lowered a whole step, or double flatted. It's enharmonic to the major 6th of a scale.

You may see various descriptions in a chord suffix that are self-explanatory, such as "C6(no3)." This would obviously indicate a 6th chord with no 3rd. The scale degrees in a chord like this would be 1–5–6. Any chord suffix containing "(no3)" or "(no5)" means exactly what it indicates.

There are more chords to dissect, but this is the majority of them without getting into poly chords. Also, it's important to note that the spelling, or voicing, of a chord has a tremendous amount to do with the resonant quality of the chord as a whole. A full 13th chord (1–3–5–♭7–9–11–13) can sound a bit dissonant if played in one voicing, but it could sound more spacious and harmonically dimensional in another voicing.

CHORD SPELLING
(ADVANCED STUDY)

Close Voicing

A **close voicing** is a voicing of a chord with the notes stacked in their closest possible position. An example would be a Cmaj7 chord that is voiced with scale tones from bottom to top: 1–3–5–7 (C–E–G–B stacked on the staff). This is also sometimes called "four-way close voicing."

Try finding as many close voicings on the guitar that you can for the various chords in the previous Chord Symbol Dictionary. It's hard to play four-way close voicings on the guitar because the notes are so close to each other in pitch.

Open Voicing

An **open voicing** is the stacking of a chord with some "space" between the notes, meaning they are not necessarily stacked next to each other by chord scale degrees. There are many, many more open voicings of a chord then there are close voicings. In fact, there is actually only one close voicing of any one chord.

Chord Inversions

A **chord inversion** is a respelling of a chord voicing, with the same notes appearing in different octaves. One example is done by taking the lowest note of a chord and moving it up an octave. Below is an example of a close-voiced Cmaj7 with this inversion technique. As you can see, 1st inversion has the 3rd as the lowest note, 2nd inversion has the 5th as the lowest note, and 3rd inversion has the 7th as the lowest note.

| Cmaj7 | Cmaj7/E | Cmaj7/G | Cmaj7/B |
| Root Position | 1st Inversion | 2nd Inversion | 3rd Inversion |

After you find various close voicings for the chords in the Chord Symbol Dictionary, try to invert them on the guitar with the inversion technique above. Due to how the guitar is laid out, it's difficult to find many close-voice inversions because of the closeness of the scale degrees.

Drop voicings are a good solution for guitar players because they spread out the chords a little more. A drop voicing is just what it says: it takes one of the "voices" (notes) from a chord and drops it an octave. With the example of a Cmaj7 close voicing (C–E–G–B), a "drop 2" voicing would take the second note *from the top* of the chord and drop it one octave. A "drop 3" voicing takes the third note (from the top) of the chord and drops it one octave, and so on.

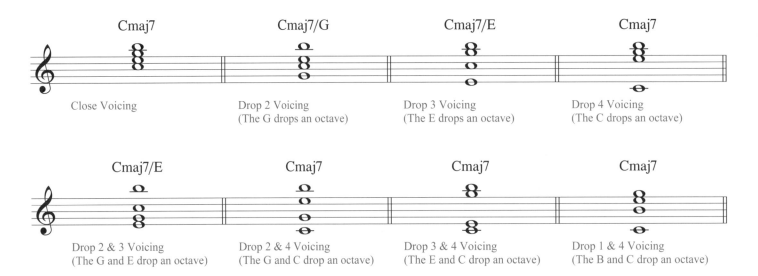

Try experimenting with drop voicings with some of the close voicings of various chords.

Another technique for creating inversions would be to do the reverse of the drop technique and raise a particular voice an octave. Perhaps I will call these "reverse drop voicings."

When I believe I'm making up terminology, it's only because I don't know of any conventional terminology that means the same thing, but it may exist; there may be conventional terminology out there.

Another, and very practical, way of creating chord inversions on the guitar is to take any chord and raise each note to the next voicing in the chord. Here is an example of an Fmaj7 chord that is voiced 1–7–3–5 from bottom to top:

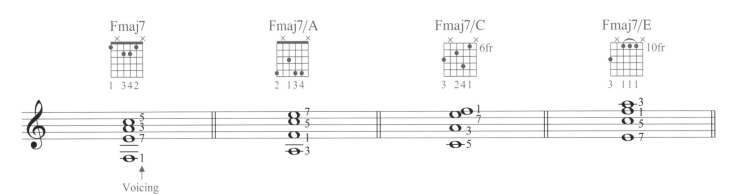

By inverting this chord with this technique, the first note in the chord (low F, the root) would move up to the next chord scale degree, which is the major 3rd, or A. So, you can see in the second chord that the 3rd, A, is in the bass.

The second note in the original chord (E, or the M7) would move up to the next chord scale degree, which would be the 1, or F. So, you can see in the second chord, the second note is F.

The third note in the original chord (the M3, or A) would move up to the next chord scale degree, which would be the P5, or C. And the top note of the chord (the 5th, or C) would move up to the next chord scale degree, which would be the M7, or E. The resultant inversion is an Fmaj7/A, and it's voiced 3–1–5–7.

The next inversion would take the 3 to the 5, the 1 to the 3, the 5 to the 7, and the 7 to the 1, resulting in an Fmaj7/C, etc.

You can apply this inversion technique to virtually any chord on the guitar (or otherwise), and you can also reverse invert chords. A "reverse inversion" would take each voicing and drop it to the next lowest scale degree of the chord.

Try taking all the chords you know and do full inversions of them. If you do this enough, the neck will open up like mad for you. The ultimate goal in this is to be able to take any chord you play and see it instantly on the neck in all its inversions.

Exercise

If you're into it, creating your own unique chord library is a great way to get excited about the sound of interesting chords you find under your fingers. Here are a few things to try:

1. Write 3–5 ways of playing each of the chords in the Chord Symbol Library.

2. Now figure out the inversions for all of them.

3. Try writing no less than one cool new chord that you were unaware of every day, put them in your private chord library, and write a little progression with them.

CHORDS
(EXPERIENTIAL STUDY CONTINUED)

As mentioned, whenever you are using your analytical brain to memorize finger structures, chord names, voicings, intervals, etc., always take the time to shift your focus to the other side of the brain and experience things on a deeper level. This is done by listening deeply, with no thought about the academics. Memorizing the sound quality and personality of a chord is more vital than understanding the academics of it.

WRITING MUSIC
(ACADEMIC STUDY)

You may decide that you never want to read or write music, and that's fine. But it's probably a good idea to at least understand the basics. Having said that, I have found that understanding music notation has the potential to open a type of creativity that you could not find if you didn't know music notation.

Written music is beautiful; it looks like art! And if you understand this language, you can write music that brings together large groups of people to audibly manifest what was lurking in your imagination. It's an infinite tool for musical expression. Here's a chart of basic note values:

NOTE VALUES						
Note	Name	Value	Bar	Rest	Dotted Note	Dotted Value
𝅜	Double Whole Note	8 beats	𝄴 𝅜	𝄺	𝅜·	12 beats
o	Whole Note	4 beats	𝄴 o	𝄻	o·	6 beats
♩	Half Note	2 beats	𝄴 ♩ ♩	𝄼	♩·	3 beats
♩	Quarter Note	1 beat	𝄴 ♩ ♩ ♩ ♩	𝄽	♩·	1.5 beats
♪	Eighth Note	1/2 beat	𝄴 ♫♫♫♫ ♫♫♫♫	𝄾	♪·	3/4 beat
♬	Sixteenth Note	1/4 beat	𝄴 ♬♬♬♬ ♬♬♬♬ ♬♬♬♬	𝄿	♬·	3/8 beat
𝅘𝅥𝅲	Thirty-second Note	1/8 beat	𝄴 𝅘𝅥𝅲...	𝅀	𝅘𝅥𝅲·	3/16 beat
𝅘𝅥𝅳	Sixty-fourth Note	1/16 beat	𝄴 𝅘𝅥𝅳...	𝅁	𝅘𝅥𝅳·	3/32 beat

Experiment by grabbing various types of written music and reading through the rhythms. Practice sight-singing the rhythms. Also take a few pieces of music and read them over and over until you have them down perfectly.

Another exercise would be to fill 5–10 pages of manuscript paper with various rhythms and then read them back until you can get through all the pages perfectly. At first, this all may seem like a lot of work, but if you want to have an intimate understanding of rhythmic notation—and it really only takes a little while to master it—just stick with it. This will vastly improve your inner drummer. The goal is worth it.

POLYRHYTHMS

Polyrhythms, also called **cross-rhythms** or **tuplets**, are the simultaneous combination of contrasting rhythms. The simplest example of this is an **eighth-note triplet**, wherein three eighth notes are evenly spaced over two eighth notes (or one beat).

What the above is essentially saying is: play three eighth notes evenly in the space of two eighth notes. The reason an eighth-note triplet only has one beam is because it is within the number of notes that would fit over two eighth notes but is less than the next beamed grouping, which is 16th notes (four per beat).

It's worth mentioning that the bracket that accompanies a polyrhythm is optional for groups of notes that are beamed together. If a polyrhythm contains note values that are not beamed to each other, it's a good idea to use brackets for clarity. I use them quite often. Also, the bracket and the tuplet number should always appear on the beamed side of a polyrhythmic grouping, unless space doesn't permit it.

A **quarter-note triplet** is three quarter notes spaced evenly over two quarter notes:

A **16th-note quintuplet** is five 16th notes spaced evenly over four 16th notes (or one beat). You would not beam these notes with eighth-note beaming because they exceed four divisions (16th-note division) of a beat.

An **eighth-note quintuplet** is five notes spaced evenly over four eighth notes (or two beats).

There are various ways to write polyrhythms. When writing unorthodox-type polyrhythms, the more information you give, the easier it will be for someone who's reading your music to understand what you want. It's not uncommon to use ratios and note durations in a polyrhythmic bracket that indicate the number of notes in the polyrhythm, the note duration they cover in the meter, and the kind of note duration. For example, what the example below is saying is: play five eighth notes evenly over the space of four eighth notes, or, as in the second grouping, play five eighth notes in the space of two quarter notes. They are synonymous.

Here is an example of various polyrhythms and how they would essentially line up:

POLYRHYTHMS (ADVANCED)

As you can imagine, you can construct some pretty crazy polyrhythmic situations. When you put polyrhythms inside polyrhythms, they are usually called "nested tuplets." Below are some wild examples pulled from transcriptions I did while working for Frank Zappa. These examples have guitar and drums transcribed.

Example 1

Example 2

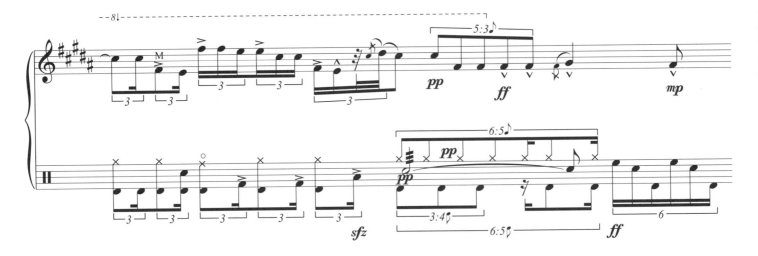

Example 3

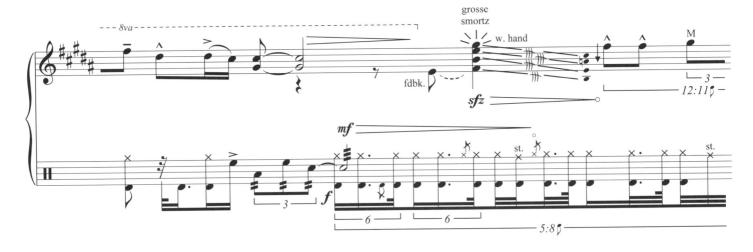

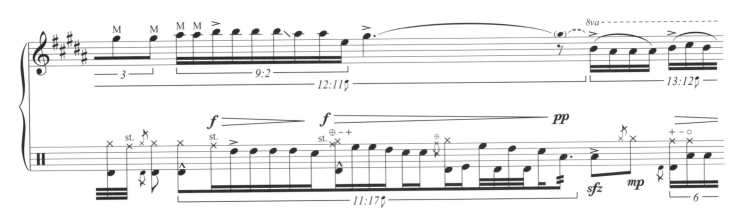

Tuplet Terminology

Here is some tuplet terminology for the number of notes that appear in a polyrhythm (I'm sure I made some of these up, but they make quirky sense).

Duplet: 2

Triplet: 3

Quadruplet: 4 (16th notes)

Quintuplet: 5

Sextuplet: 6 (16th-note triplets)

Septuplet: 7

Octuplet: 8 (32nd notes)

Neptuplet: 9

Decatuplet: 10

Undatuplet: 11

Duodecatuplet: 12 (32nd-note triplets)

Tridecatuplet: 13

Quadradecatuplet: 14

Quindadecatuplet: 15

Sexadecatuplet: 16 (64th notes)

Septadecatuplet: 17

Octadecatuplet: 18

Neptadecatuplet: 19

Vigintatuplet: 20

Vigintunatuplet: 21

Vigindupotuplet: 22

Vigintriptotuplet: 23

Viginquadratuplet: 24 (64th-note triplets)

Most of the above is not necessarily theoretical, because in certain types of contemporary music, you may see something like 23 over four beats, a "vigintriptotuplet," or "23 over 4."

An interesting way to create a unique groove is to have various rhythmic instruments play multiple polyrhythms at the same time but just accenting partials of the polyrhythms. In the example below, there are various polyrhythms being played against each other, but the notes within the polyrhythms are accented in various groups. Using this technique can create some pretty interesting groove feelings.

The polyrhythmic terminology I use for two rhythms of uneven proportion playing against each other is "duo-rhythmic." If there are three, "tripto-rhythmic." Four polyrhythms going against each other would be "quadra-rhythmic," five would be "quinto-rhythmic," six would be "sexto-rhythmic," seven would be "septo-rhythmic," eight would be "octo-rhythmic," nine would be "nepto-rhythmic" (I think I made that up), etc. The example below, then, would be considered "quadra-rhythmic."

When exploring polyrhythms, it's not uncommon for them to feel unnatural at first. The academic study of them includes practicing various types of polyrhythms until they feel even and natural to you. One exercise in particular that can be very helpful is as follows:

1. Practice tapping out or singing the following for a few minutes each or longer. Do each example until it feels totally even and natural. Try these examples at 3–4 different tempos, from very slow to as fast as you can sing them evenly.

A. Triplets:

B. Quintuplets:

C. Sextuplets:

D. Septuplets:

E. Neptuplets:

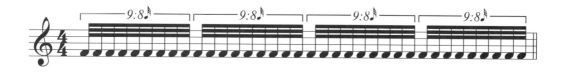

Each beamed group of the previous polyrhythms is performed over one full beat. A helpful thing to do is subdivide the counting of them. For example, divide the quintuplets into groups of 2 and 3, sextuplets into 3 and 3, septuplets into 4 and 3, and neptuplets into 3, 3, and 3.

After working on single-beat polyrhythms until they feel natural to you, try beating out the following example. Remember to make each beat even, and the polyrhythmic subdivisions within them should be even, too. Try this at various tempos and try writing several pages of a mixture of these types of rhythms, working them until they feel natural.

After you have these basic polyrhythms feeling natural, work to feel them over two beats:

1. **Quarter-Note Triplets:**

2. **Eighth-Note Quintuplets:**

3. **Eighth-Note Septuplets:**

4. **16th-Note Neptuplets:**

5. **16th-Note 11s, or "undatuplets":**

6. **16th-Note 13s, or "tridecatuplets":**

It's impractical to count these higher tuplets without subdividing. Experiment with the subdivisions that feel best to you. For instance, the groups of 13 can be subdivided into 5, 5, and 3—as long as they are even.

Once you get the feeling of polyrhythms over two beats, try writing five pages of all the polyrhythms you know and then read them back.

If you find this challenge interesting and rewarding—and it's very rewarding when it all syncs up—try variations of polyrhythms over three quarter notes, doing the same types of exercises. Then move onto polys over four beats, then five beats, etc.

POLYRHYTHMS (EXPERIENTIAL STUDY)

The idea here is to break through conventional rhythmic conditioning and into the vast and liquid world of polyrhythms. If you stick with it, there will come a time when they feel very natural to you. This will loosen up the inelasticity of your inner clock, and this will flow into your playing, making it more "rubato" and engaging. But they have to feel natural to you just like quarter notes or eighth notes might feel now. In the beginning, when you start locking into these quirky rhythms, there may be a rigidity in the way you feel them. But, after a while, this will loosen up, and you will notice it in the fluidity of your playing.

TIME SIGNATURES (ACADEMIC)

When reading a **time signature**, the bottom number tells you the note value that the top number is based on, while the top number tells you how many of the bottom-number note values are in a bar. So, in 4/4 time, there is the equivalent of four quarter notes to the bar.

Another way of putting it: the top number of a time signature tells you how many beats are in one measure, and the bottom number tells you what kind of note is counted as one beat.

The bottom note will most commonly be an even number that points to its rhythmic counterpart. The most common bottom numbers in a time signature are 2, 4, 8, 16, and 32. It's extremely rare to see any other numbers, with the exception of particular contemporary music that usually needs an explanation in the piece's performance notes.

The top number could be practically anything. In something like 5/8 time, the time signature is telling you that there is the equivalent of five eighth notes to one bar. With a time signature of something like 13/16, you're being told that each bar contains the equivalent of 13 16th notes. Of course, each bar can be divided by any combination of note durations, as long as they do not add up to less than or more than the equivalent of what the time signature is dictating.

Common Time: 4/4 Meter

The most common meter in music is 4/4. It's so common that its other name is **common time**, and the two numbers in the time signature are often replaced by the letter "C." In 4/4, the stacked numbers tell you that each measure contains the equivalent of four quarter-note beats. So, to count 4/4 meter, each time you tap the beat, you're tapping the equivalent of one quarter note.

Waltz Time: 3/4 Meter

Perhaps the second most common meter is 3/4. Each measure has the equivalent of three quarter-note beats within it.

March Time: 2/4 Meter

This meter, 2/4, has the equivalent of two quarter notes per bar.

Of course, you can have any practical number in the numerator to create various time signatures such as 5/4, 6/4, 7/4, 8/4, 9/4, etc. If a written time signature seems impractical, there's probably a better way of writing it.

Duple, Triple, Quadruple, Simple, and Compound Meter

These classifications result from the relationship between the time signature and the actual pulse of a bar of music, or its meter. **Meter** refers to recurring patterns and accents that give a piece of music its pulse. The various meters (simple, compound, duple, triple, quadruple) and various combinations of these terms are designated by the way the notes are grouped rhythmically within a bar, based on its time signature.

Simple Meter

Time signatures can be classified into a certain meter. **Simple meter** means the note value that makes up the pulse of a bar of music can be divided by 2 without resulting in a dotted note as the pulse. The time signature in simple meter will always have a 2, 3, 4, etc., as the top number.

Compound Meter

Compound meter means the note value that makes up the pulse of a bar of music has a dotted value to it.

Duple, Triple, and Quadruple Meter

These refer to the number of pulses in a measure. **Duple meter** would have two pulses, **triple meter** would have three pulses, and **quadruple meter** would have four pulses.

Duple, triple, and quadruple meter can each be considered compound or simple, depending on the time signature and the pulse of the bar. Following are examples of various combinations.

METER CHART			
Kind	**Time Signature**	**Pulse Division**	**Best Division**
Simple Duple	**2/2**		
Simple Duple	**2/4**		
Simple Triple	**3/8**		
Simple Triple	**3/4**		
Simple Quadruple	**4/4**		
Compound Duple	**6/16**		
Compound Duple	**6/8**		
Compound Duple	**6/4**		
Compound Triple	**9/16**		
Compound Triple	**9/8**		

(chart continues on next page)

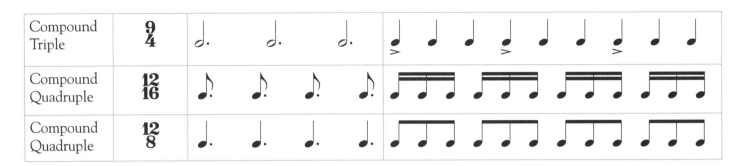

Compound Triple	**9 / 4**											
Compound Quadruple	**12 / 16**											
Compound Quadruple	**12 / 8**											

Many other time signatures fall within the meter considerations of the previous chart and have either a simple (divisible by 2) or compound (divisible by 3) allocation. Some may be theoretical but do exist: sextuple time, octuple time (double quadruple), double octuple time, quintuple time, septuple time, double quintuple time, double septuple time, triple quintuple time, quintuple triple time, triple septuple time, septuple triple time, quintuple plus sextuple time, sextuple plus quintuple time, quintuple plus octuple time, and octuple plus quintuple time.

Complex (Odd) Time Signatures

Complex, or "odd," **time signatures** do not fit the usual duple, triple, or quadruple categories. Other names for odd time signatures might be "asymmetric," "irregular," or "unusual." Below are some examples of odd meter. And, as with all other meters, any combination of note values can exist within the bar as long as they add up to no less than or no more than what the time signature dictates.

TIME SIGNATURES (ADVANCED)

Composite Meter

You can get pretty creative with time signatures and rhythms. When an odd meter has subdivisions in the pulse, it can be noted as **composite meter**. The time signature of the example below is in 7/8, but the pulse is subdivided into 4+3.

Another, and perhaps more practical, way of writing a composite-meter time signature is in this example:

Various composite time signatures can be subdivided in many ways. These composite meters are not only valuable for creating unusual time signatures, but also for creating an accurate beaming pattern in the written music. This aids in the ease of reading and writing this type of time. Here's an example in 13/8:

Poly-Meter (or Poly-Metric)

Poly-meter is when you have two or more time signatures going against each other at the same time. They will eventually re-align if repeated a specific number of times. When writing poly-metric meter, I refer to multiple time signatures playing at the same time as:

Duo-Metric:	2	**Nepto-Metric:**	9	**Sexadeca-Metric:**	16
Tripto-Metric:	3	**Deca-Metric:**	10	**Septadeca-Metric:**	17
Quadra-Metric:	4	**Undeca-Metric:**	11	**Octadeca-Metric:**	18
Quinta-Metric:	5	**Duodeca-Metric:**	12	**Neptadeca-Metric:**	19
Sexto-Metric:	6	**Triptodeca-Metric:**	13	**Viginta-Metric:**	20
Septo-Metric:	7	**Quadradeca-Metric:**	14	**Vigintuno-Metric:**	21
Octo-Metric:	8	**Quintadeca-Metric:**	15	**Vigindupo-Metric:**	22
				Etc.	

The example below could be considered "quadra-metric."

GUITAR TABLATURE

Most tablature books contain an explanation of the particular tab they are using, as there are many different ways to represent the same things. What's presented here are some of the more common ways that make sense to me (not that I use tab).

Guitar **tablature** (or "tab") is a way of writing music specifically for guitar. It's perfect for those who do not read music, and, in a few cases, it can offer information that written notation could have trouble with. But, in some ways, it's inferior to written music. Unfortunately, the guitar is one of the hardest instruments to sight-read music notation on because of the way the strings are laid out and how that relates to finding the best fingerings for a musical passage. Most guitar players need to "learn" the music, but there are a handful of excellent sight-readers out there (Steve Lukather is one that comes to mind). Tab offers a solution for finding the best fret positions where a piece of music could be played on the guitar. This is one of tab's plusses. There are also quite a few articulations that are specific to guitar tab that can be used.

Tab has six horizontal lines that represent the six strings on the guitar. The top line is the thinnest (first) string, and the lowest line represents the thickest (sixth) string. The larger numbers that are placed on the lines tell you what fret to play a note on. In some cases, you will see a smaller number next to the larger numbers; these indicate which fret-hand finger to use. You will only play the strings with numbers on them. If a string has no number, don't play it. A "0" means that a string is played open, with no fingers pressing down on the string.

It's worth it to mention that seven-string guitar tab has seven lines in its tab, and eight-string has eight. This is obvious but… I'm just sayin'.

GUITAR TAB

61

As you read tab from left to right, the linear aspect represents time, but there is no real indication for the exact time values of each note. To remedy this, you may see tab written with the rhythmic notation underneath the tab as follows:

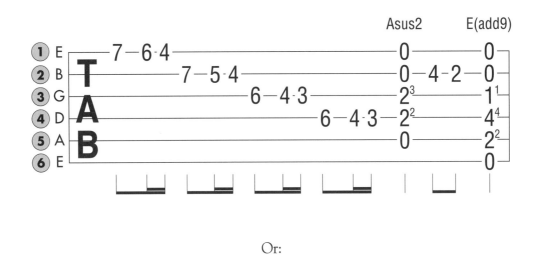

Or:

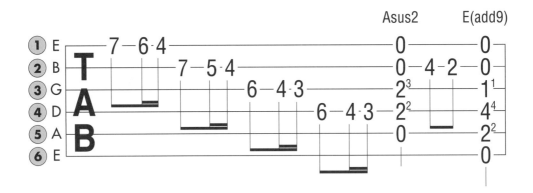

If tab is accompanied by written music in a staff above it, there's no real need to include the note rhythms within the tab, as they will be indicated on the staff.

GUITAR TAB ARTICULATION AND ORNAMENTATION

Many of the same articulations and ornaments that are used in music manuscript writing can be applied to guitar tab. But tab also offers some unique articulations for guitar.

1. **Hammer-On:** When a lower-number fret precedes a higher-number fret, and they are connected by a slur, it indicates that the note is struck (picked) on the lower fret and the next note is hammered. It's not uncommon to see a small "h" over the slur, which means "hammer." Sometimes the "h" is represented without the slur, but it means the same thing: hammer the note.

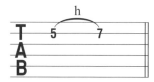

2. **Pull-Off:** Conversely, when a higher-number fret precedes a lower-number fret, and they are connected by a slur, it indicates a pull-off. It's not uncommon to see a small "p" over the slur, which stands for "pull-off."

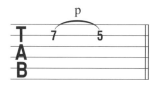

3. **Slide:** Two notes connected by a straight line on the same string indicates a slide. If the first fret is lower than the second, then the slide line will be slanted upward a bit, indicating it's a slide *up* to a note. If the first fret is higher than the second, then the slide line will be slanted downward a bit to indicate a slide *down* to a note.

4. **Bend:** A bend indication is an arched line with an arrow at the end that is pointing upward. The word "full" or number "1" means to bend a whole step, and "1/2" indicates to bend only a half step, or one fret.

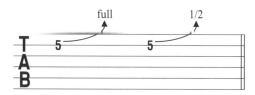

5. **Pre-Bend:** An arched arrow pointing downward indicates a pre-bend. The bend line points to the target note.

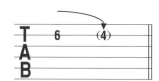

Here are some obvious ornaments:

6. **Vibrato:**

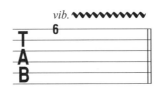

7. **Bend Hat:**

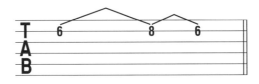

8. **Release Bend:**

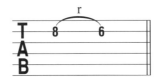

9. **Palm Mute:**

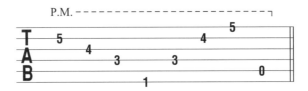

10. **Let Ring:**

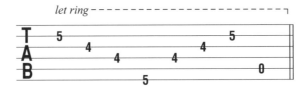

11. **Hold the Bend:**

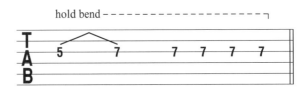

12. **Up Picking:**

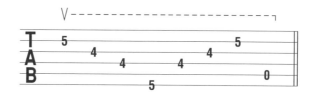

13. **Down Picking:**

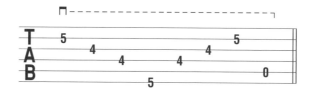

14. **Trills:** Trills can be indicated in various ways, as shown below. The parenthetical "5" next to the "3" in the first example indicates what fret to trill on. The second example indicates to trill a half step (one fret) flat, and the third example a half step (one fret) sharp.

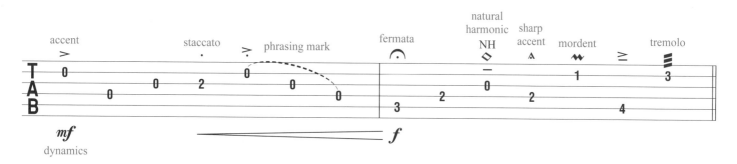

Various manuscript articulations can be used, although they are not common in tab. The red words indicate the names of the markings.

COMPOSING MUSIC

Composing music is a wildly creative process, and there are a host of tools that a composer can use to decorate their music (giving it color, phrasing, dynamics, etc.) that a music reader will understand. Here are a few music writing tools that can help if you take writing to another level...

Tempo

The tempo of a piece of music is usually written in the top left of the part, or score, either directly over the clef or slightly to the right of the clef. The tempo is usually represented by a note value equaling a particular metronome marking such as:

♩ = **120**   In this example, the quarter-note beat equals 120 beats per minute (**bpm**).

♩. = **127**   In the next example, a dotted quarter note equals 127 bpm. You would usually see something like this in 6/8 (compound duple time) or 9/8 (compound triple time), etc.

♪ = **78**   In this example, the eighth note is equal to 78 bpm.

Swing! ♫ = ♩♪   Next is a "swing" indicator. It basically means that the eighth notes in the music should be played as if they were an eighth-note triplet with the first note having a quarter-note value of the triplet and the second having an eighth-note value.

Instead of writing an actual bpm tempo marking, many composers decide to use the relative equivalent Italian words that give an idea of a basic tempo. There are various iterations in between these markings, as well.

- **Grave:** very slow (25–45 bpm)
- **Largo:** broadly (40–60 bpm)
- **Lento:** slowly (45–60 bpm)
- **Adagio:** slowly with great expression (66–76 bpm)
- **Andante:** at a walking pace (76–108 bpm)
- **Moderato:** at a moderate speed (108–120 bpm)
- **Allegro:** fast, quickly, and bright (120–156 bpm)
- **Vivace:** lively and fast (156–176 bpm)
- **Presto:** very, very fast (168–200 bpm)

Tempo Alterations

There are ways to indicate tempo alterations in your music. Here are the two you may see the most:

- **Ritardando:** slow down
- **Accelerando:** speed up

Tempo and Metric Modulations

A **tempo modulation** is an indication in the music that gives a new, specific time value to a flowing passage based on the time value that came before it.

A tempo is a term that is usually used after a tempo alteration and indicates to return to the previous tempo (the one before the tempo modulation occurred).

Metric modulations define an instant change in the tempo of the piece based on note values that were in place prior to the metric modulation.

This example indicates a metric modulation in which the value of the eighth note from an eighth-note triplet in the previous bar is now equal to the value of a "regular" (or "straight") eighth note in the subsequent bar. The tempo would be 50% faster in the subsequent bar.

In this example, the 16th note of a quintuplet in the previous bar is equal to a regular 16th note in the subsequent bar, so the subsequent music will be 20% faster than the previous tempo.

As you can imagine, one can use any kind of note-value proportion to create a tempo modulation.

Repetition Signs

There are various ways to notate repetitions in music.

When a single beat is repeated, regardless if the beat has a chord, one note, or multiple notes of the same value within it, it is indicated with a single, thick, slanting slash placed between the second and fourth staff lines.

If the beat is made up of even 16th notes, two slashes are required, and 32nd notes require three slashes.

Beats consisting of mixed values are abbreviated by using double slashes accompanied by two dots:

The repetition of an entire measure (whether it consisted of mixed rhythms or not) is indicated by a single slanted slash with two dots on each side, as in the example below.

If a bar is to be repeated twice, it can be indicated with the symbol below.

Repeat signs are common and indicate that the music is to be repeated inside the repeat signs one time only (unless otherwise indicated).

A **first and second ending** is an indication to play up to the repeat sign (under the first-ending indication) and then return to the previous repeat sign and play through the music again, but, when arriving at the first-ending indication the second time, the player needs to jump to the second ending instead of playing the first ending.

D.S., or **dal segno**, means "from the sign." It directs the player to return to a spot earlier in the music that's marked by the 𝄋 sign. If the marking says **D.S. al Coda**, the player is supposed to play from the 𝄋 to a "To Coda" marking, then jump to the Coda section at the end of the music. This is the Coda marking: ⊕

Articulations

Articulations are ornaments that you can use in notation to tell the reader how to attack a note. Here is a list of simple dynamic articulations that work well when applied to guitar music:

NOTE ARTICULATIONS		
Symbol	**Name**	**How to play the note**
	Staccato	Short, light
	Tenuto	Long, apply pressure to note
	Accent	Hard for full value of note
	Accent (housetop)	Harder and more percussive
	Accent with staccato	Hard and short
	Accent with tenuto	Hard and long

Dynamics

Dynamics are a great way to add dimension to your music. Here's a list of the dynamic ranges you will most likely be working in, along with the Italian terminology and the English description:

DYNAMICS CHART		
Dynamic Sign	**Italian**	**English Description**
pppp	*pianississississimo*	Very, very, very soft
ppp	*pianissississimo*	Very, very soft
pp	*pianissimo*	Very soft
p	*piano*	Soft
mp	*mezzo piano*	Moderately soft
mf	*mezzo forte*	Moderately loud
f	*forte*	Loud
ff	*fortissimo*	Very loud
fff	*fortississimo*	Very, very loud
ffff	*fortissississimo*	Very, very, very loud

Some dynamic markings can act similar to accents and take on the terms **sforzando**, **forzando** (or **forzato**), and **sforzato**. They are used in their abbreviated form, as seen below. There are basically three principal degrees of these accent terms graded in intensity and force. They are used within their corresponding dynamic in the music. The chart below shows these dynamic markings, along with their equivalent accent marks.

DYNAMIC ACCENTS								
Sforzando Accent attack of note			**Forzando or Forzato** Sharper, more percussive accent at attack of note			**Sforzato** Percussive accent for full note value		
Marking	Accent equivalent	Dynamic levels used in	Marking	Accent equivalent	Dynamic levels used in	Marking	Accent equivalent	Dynamic levels used in
sf	>	*ppppp* to *f*	*fz*	∧	*mf* or *f*	*sfz*	△	*mf* or *f*
sff	>	*ff*	*ffz*	∧	*ff*	*sffz*	△	*ff*
sfff	>	*fff*	*fffz*	∧	*fff*	*sfffz*	△	*fff*

fp   Means **fortepiano** and indicates loud then soft.

sfp   Means **sforzando piano** and indicates to accent the note and then play soft.

There are multiple combinations of various dynamics that can be combined to give specific direction to the way a note or passage is performed. You may see some abbreviated accent dynamic markings that are not written in the table above, but once you understand these dynamic signs and what they are referring to, combining various dynamics will make practical sense.

COMPOSING MUSIC CONTINUED

There are various other articulation and expression tools that can be used in written music to give your music dimension and depth. Here are some notational tools that can aid in composition:

Crescendo

This sign indicates a gradual increase in the volume of a passage. It's sometimes referred to as a "hairpin" or **cresc.**

Decrescendo

This sign indicates a gradual decrease in volume of a passage.

Here's an example using both:

Octave Sign

Sometimes a written passage is either so high or so low that it requires stacks of ledger lines. An octave sign placed over a bar, a note, or an entire section of music indicates to play the note or passage an octave higher (**8va**) or an octave lower (**8vb**) than where it's written. The term **loco** means to return to the octave the music is written in.

15ma, when placed above the staff, indicates that a particular note or passage is to be played two octaves higher than where it's written, or two octaves lower than where it's written if the **15ma** sign is written below the staff.

GUITAR HARMONICS

Perhaps a lot has been written about the notation of guitar harmonics, but I have yet to see a clearly defined notation that specifically denotes both artificial harmonics and natural harmonics and also indicates the exact harmonic note being sounded. I venture to clarify this phenomenon with the following notation.

Natural Harmonics

A **natural harmonic** is the kind of harmonic that is produced by lightly touching a string over a particular fret and striking the note, then quickly pulling your finger away from the note to let it ring. The result is a natural harmonic. There are various places on the guitar neck where natural harmonics are produced relatively easily and the resultant pitches have a nice, rounded bell-like tone to them. On the guitar, over the fifth, seventh, and 12th frets (and the 19th and 24th frets in the second octave) are the easiest places on the neck to produce natural harmonics. Natural harmonics can be produced over various other frets but it gets more difficult to produce a good-sounding harmonic over any fret other than the fifth, seventh, or 12th... unless you're Jeff Beck!

The way I notate natural harmonics is with the written note indicating what note would sound if you pressed on that particular fret. The small circle floating on a stem above the note is the actual tone of the harmonic that's produced. Using tab when writing harmonics gives a clearer picture of exactly which fret to play over to produce the harmonic.

In the example below, you will notice that, when you strike a natural harmonic over the 12th fret, the harmonic produces the same pitch as if you fretted the 12th fret.

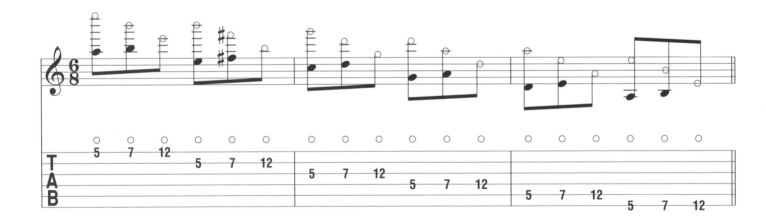

Artificial Harmonics

Artificial harmonics, or "pinch" harmonics, are usually produced by choking up on the pick (sort of squeezing it by pinching your fingers a bit) and "pinching" the string with both the pick and a little bit of finger/thumb flesh at various places in the area over the pickups (or soundhole on acoustics), while the left hand either frets a note or uses an open string.

Artificial harmonics can be more difficult to produce than natural harmonics. Much of it has to do with the note you are fretting and where you actually place the pinch on the string with the pick. A lot of experimenting will help, as there are myriad combinations of notes and pinch locations that create all sorts of squealing delights—just ask Zakk Wylde. He can produce artificial harmonics virtually anywhere—with stunning accuracy!

I notate artificial harmonics in a similar way as natural harmonics, with the exception being the notehead of the sounding harmonic, which is diamond-shaped instead of a little circle. Also, being that artificial harmonics have a tendency to create very high overtones, it's not uncommon to use an octave sign over the harmonic, but the octave sign is only referring to the sounding pitch of the harmonic itself (the regular note is played as written). It can be a challenge to find the right spot to pinch the string with the right hand in order to get the harmonic to come out consistently.

Keep in mind that the guitar is a transposing instrument, so everything you play is sounding an octave lower than where it's written, including the harmonics.

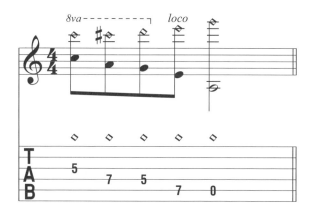

READING GUITAR RHYTHM

Most often, guitar rhythm is written with the chord tab and chord name placed over the bar, and any particular rhythm strumming indicated in "slash" notation in the bar.

In the example below, you would play an E chord for four beats and strum basically any way you feel is appropriate for the groove of the song.

The following example shows the note duration in note values in the top staff and "slash" strum notation in the second staff.

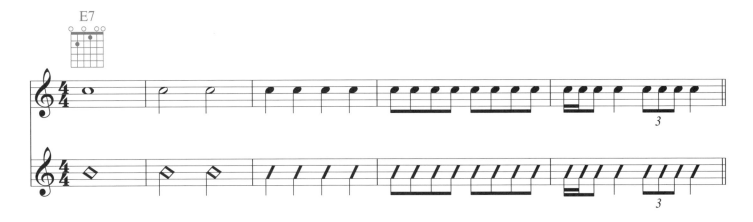

Here are some examples of strumming notation:

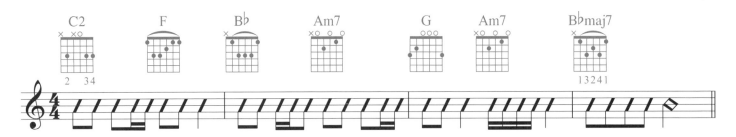

The following example shows various ways you might see tab and notation joined together. At the top of the staff is the chord tab; under it are the rhythmic strumming indications for the chords. Below that, the second staff shows the actual chords written out in notation. The "X" noteheads represent a muted strum, and under the notation are strum directions.

⊓ = downstrum

V = upstrum

In the very bottom staff is the tab for the changes.

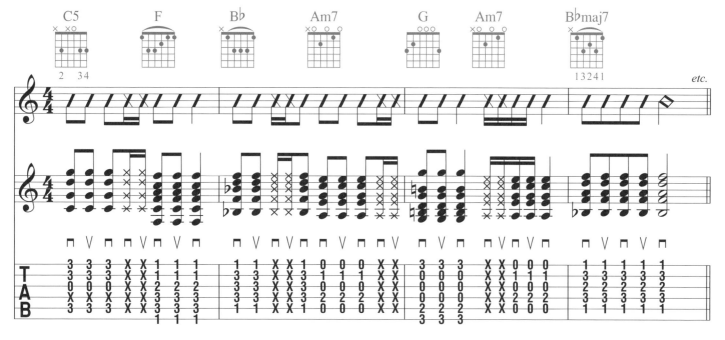

Here are some things to try:

- Take those delicious chords you notated in your private chord library and, in the next hour, use strumming notation to write five songs or progressions. Use different time signatures and utilize odd meter, compound and simple, and the various tools outlined in this section. Experiment with different tempos, meters, time signatures, and grooves.

- Record your songs to a drum machine, or build a track in your computer with samples, or just record the changes, or have a friend play them live. Recording them with a band is perhaps the most communicative way to do it.

- Even if you are not sure which scale to use when soloing, if you listen intensely to the chords being played, your fingers will find notes that work.

- Listen to your favorite kind of rhythm playing and emulate it. Listening to cultural music that you may not normally listen to can expand your rhythmic horizons. Check out some of the following music, invest yourself in the grooves, and then emulate them on the guitar. Examples of this music can be found on the Internet: ska, reggae, calypso, Caribbean, blues, metal, jazz, Western, R&B, waltz, Bulgarian, Spanish, salsa, polka, and Creole are all available. Go to the Internet and search for "Cultural Music." There are endless lists of amazing and unique styles of music that you can research and pull from.

RHYTHM (EXPERIENTIAL STUDY)

As mentioned, there's usually a period of time when you are learning something that you may have to apply a little discipline (although passion is a better substitute). There's that period when you have to work things out. The more you review the fundamentals, the easier they will be within your grasp. I suggest mastering these fundamentals the best you can. You will know when you have mastered something when it feels natural to you. What you are looking for is the feeling of simplicity, ease, non-thinking doing, elegance, otherworldly bliss while performing, and total freedom.

There's a sweet spot that happens where you transition from having to think about what you're doing to *being* what you are doing. That may sound abstract, but you will know what I mean when you get there. You may already be there. You probably are on some things. You are already there on many things in your life that you had to first hone your skills at by working and focusing on the academics before they became natural to you. Perhaps some examples are: driving a car, riding a bicycle, tying your shoes, cooking, reading and writing, and *sex*! Whatever it is, there was a period when you went from having to learn about it, think about it, and practice it, to the point of it feeling organic, free-flowing, and sort of magical while you are doing it.

To get there on the guitar, you will need to apply continuous repetition over and over and over and over while keeping your attention focused on whatever it is you are doing and making it sound like music. By keeping your attention on what you are doing while you are honing your skills, you will find yourself morphing what you are playing until it sounds like what you want it to sound like. But you need to keep a picture in your head of what you are striving for. If you can do this, then every time you come back to the instrument to play the same thing, you will notice an increase in the ease of playing it. Even if what you are attempting is wildly difficult, if you start slow and get every aspect of it sounding good, there will come a time when you will find yourself not having to think about how to do it. You will simply become it.

At some point, you will pick up your instrument and that difficult thing that you were thinking was so impossible will feel natural and easy; it will flow with an elegance and ease that feels as though you've always owned it, and it will seem impossible to you to recall how difficult it was before. When you get to this point, keep in mind that you can still go deeper into it. It doesn't matter how well you can play it. If you continue to apply your intense attention as you play it, deeper levels of what it can offer will start coming onto your radar.

This practice will flow into other things you do, such as performing live with others. When you're playing your guitar, whether it's by yourself, while doing a show, jamming with some friends, or performing for 30,000 people, there's that elusive state of mind one can reach that is open, clear, and in the moment, and you're listening deeply to everything going on around you and responding instantly with inspired, and sometimes quite extraordinary, things—when all the technique, theory, and academics are in your peripheral, and not at the forefront; when you are so locked with the groove that it saturates your whole being; when ever-unfolding, unique sounds, melodies, phrasings, or chords are just flowing from your fingers in what seems like "graceful magic on tip toes;" where there are no thoughts or doubts, just pure awareness, ease, deep relaxation, nonresistance, precision, lucidity, and flexibility. I call that state of mind "The Ultra Zone." And it's yours to have. As a matter of fact, you already have it. You just have to find it, and many already have. If it resonates with the audience, they'll go there with you.

THE GROOVE

All of the aforementioned stuff about rhythm, notation, meter, time signatures, polyrhythms, etc., are all the fundamental tools at your disposal for making your own unique musical universe. But, when it comes to rhythm, of the utmost importance is that you learn how to feel it deeply. The best way to do this is to *listen* to the groove that's happening around you, or in your head, and embracing it with your whole being. Try syncing with the drummer; not just time-wise, but "psycho-metrically."

The only way to do this effectively is to relax, be still inside, and listen deeply. Relaxing is the key to virtually all ills, but I'm not referring to just relaxing your body. Your body will never be able to relax unless you can relax your mind. But what does "relax your mind" mean? I am referring to the relaxing of the usual compulsive thinking that can accompany a person all day. The only way to do this is to focus your attention on something else once you notice that the quality of the thought you are focusing on is negative and destructive to your peace.

Here's something that you can focus on if you find yourself in a state of disarray. This works every time. It's an instant peace-bringer. It can be applied to virtually any situation in life (or thoughts in your head that you may be stuck on) that is causing you concern, fear, nervousness, impatience, frustration, anger, etc. And here it is:

Relax and Breathe!

Try taking your attention out of your head and putting it into the energy field of your body and your breathing. Put your full attention on your breathing and totally relaxing your body. Take a few conscious breaths, relaxing deeper on each one. This only takes a few moments but is penetratingly powerful. This is one of the oldest known and most effective meditational techniques.

Doing this will create a sense of stillness and peace in you so when you return to the task at hand, you will have a remarkably more effective vantage point to make decisions from, or to do a task such as playing music. But this isn't something you can read about and gather knowledge from, because it is purely experiential. Only *you* can do it and experience it by aligning with the feeling of it.

CHORD SCALES
(ACADEMIC STUDY)

Chord scales are basically diatonic chords that are built on a particular scale degree. These examples are in the key of C.

Here is the C major scale in whole notes. There's no specific time signature here.

If we were to stack the notes in 3rds while staying in the key of C, we would get a string of triads and have a C major chord scale. It would look like this:

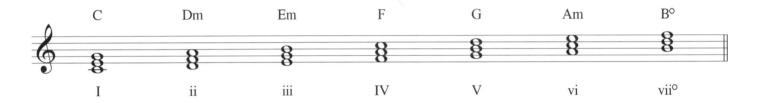

You will notice that the top line gives the name of the chord in the chord scale, and the bottom line shows the scale degree. In writing chord analyzations, it's customary to use Roman numerals. An uppercase Roman numeral indicates a major chord, and a lowercase numeral indicates a minor chord. If you were interested in writing a song in any diatonic major key, the above chord-scale outline will tell you what chords work in that key.

The reason the ii chord is a Dm chord in the key of C is because the notes—D, F, and A—outline a Dm chord. Remember from the circle of 5ths, the key of D has two sharps in it (F♯ and C♯). So, F♮ is the minor 3rd in a Dm chord.

If we take this chord-scale concept a little further and stack another diatonic 3rd on top, we will have a string of seventh chords. A dash (–) is the symbol for minor.

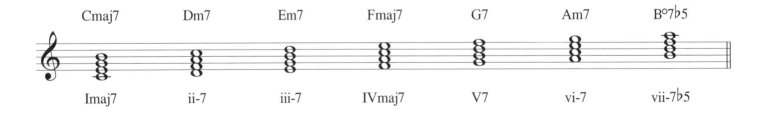

Below is a chord progression in C major. It's entirely in the key of C and the chord analysis is under the staff.

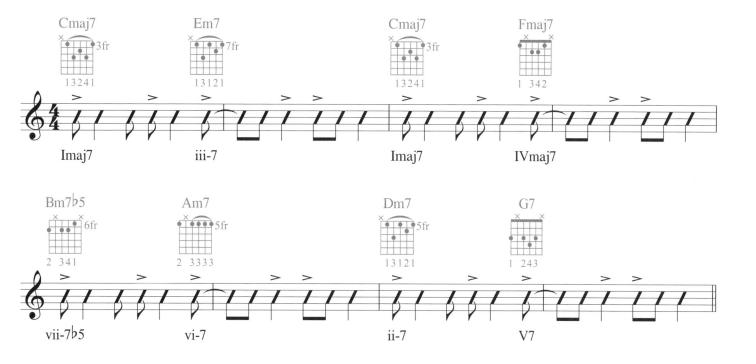

CHORD SUBSTITUTIONS

Obviously, most songs are not based on the rigidity of a diatonic chord scale. In writing music, chords can flow outside the chord scale, and there can be modulations to different keys, etc.

In music theory, **chord substitution** is the practice of using one chord in the place of another often-related chord in a chord progression. This is very prevalent in jazz music. The chord substitution should have some harmonic quality and degree of function in common with the original chord and often only differs by one or two notes.

One simple type of chord substitution is to replace a given chord with a chord that has the same function. Thus, in the simple chord progression Imaj7–ii-7–V7–Imaj7, which, in the key of C major, would be the chords Cmaj7–D-7–G7–Cmaj7, a musician can replace the Imaj7 chord with "tonic substitutes," the most widely used of which are iii-7 and vi-7 (in a major key). In this case, that would be the chords E-7 and A-7. This simple chord progression, with tonic substitutes, could become iii-7– ii-7–V7–vi-7, or E-7–D-7–G7–A-7. The musician typically uses her/his ears and sense of the musical style to determine if the chord substitution works with the melody. There are also subdominant and dominant substitutes.

Of course, you can take chord substitutions to dizzying heights that are not covered in the scope of this book. Experiment and explore. Your ears are your best guide.

MODES (ACADEMIC STUDY)

Modes can be very powerful. Once you get the simplicity of the concept of them, it all falls into place. Through the years, I've realized that most people don't know exactly what a mode is; they seem intimidated by it all because it sounds like some secret code that only the musical elite can understand, but this is far from the truth.

The names of the modes of the major scale were taken from Greek islands.

Modes are the scales that are derived by starting on any particular note within a scale but staying within the key of that scale. This is a simple explanation, but in reality, modes offer a completely different color, tonality, and emotional atmosphere when their roots are employed as the tone center.

Below are examples of the modes that are derived from the major scale—in this example, C major. There are seven. They are all technically in the key of C major, but if you made any of the root notes of these modes the main key center, you will find the tonalities are vastly different.

C Ionian (Major)	C	D	E	F	G	A	B		
D Dorian		D	E	F	G	A	B	C	
E Phrygian			E	F	G	A	B	C	D
F Lydian				F	G	A	B	C	D	E
G Mixolydian					G	A	B	C	D	E	F
A Aeolian (Natural minor)						A	B	C	D	E	F	G
B Locrian							B	C	D	E	F	G	A

Another way to look at the modes of the major scale is by their own independent scale degrees. These scale degrees are consistent with each mode, regardless of the major scale they are derived from. In the diagram below, you will find the scale name, the scale kind, the scale degrees, and the chord scale for each of the modes of the major scale.

MODES TABLE WITH CHORD SCALES										
	Name	Kind	Scale Degrees	Chord Scale						
1	Ionian	Pure Major	1–2–3–4–5–6–7	I△7	ii-7	iii-7	IV△7	V7	vi-7	vii-7♭5
2	Dorian	Minor scale with M6	1–2–♭3–4–5–6–♭7	i-7	ii-7	♭III△7	IV7	v-7	vi-7♭5	♭VII△7
3	Phrygian	Minor scale with m2	1–♭2–♭3–4–5–♭6–♭7	i-7	♭II△7	♭III7	iv-7	v-7♭5	♭VI△7	♭vii-7
4	Lydian	Major scale with aug 4th	1–2–3–♯4–5–6–7	I△7	II7	iii-7	♯iv-7♭5	V△7	vi-7	vii-7
5	Mixolydian	Major scale with m7	1–2–3–4–5–6–♭7	I7	ii-7	biii-7♭5	IV△7	v-7	vi-7	♭VII△7
6	Aeolian	Pure Minor scale	1–2–♭3–4–5–♭6–♭7	i-7	ii-7♭5	♭III△7	iv-7	v-7	♭VI△7	♭VII7
7	Locrian	Minor scale with m2, dim 5	1–♭2–♭3–4–♭5–♭6–♭7	i-7♭5	♭II△7	biii-7	iv-7	♭V△7	♭VI7	♭vii-7

MODAL PROGRESSIONS

Ionian Mode (Major Scale): First Mode of the Major Scale

Here's a simple **Ionian** (major) chord progression. Notice that the iii chord is a minor 11th, and the V chord a dominant 11th. Both of these suffixes are represented in the Roman-numeral delineation.

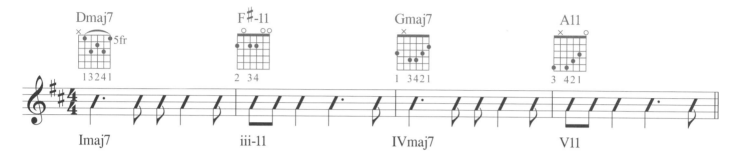

Dorian Mode: Second Mode of the Major Scale

If you play the C major scale from D to D, you are playing the D **Dorian mode**. If you made D the tonic, or root, and played the Dorian mode on it, you would hear the fantastic flavor of the Dorian mode. If you isolated a Dorian mode, the scale degrees would be 1–2–♭3–4–5–6–♭7. The Dorian mode can also be called a minor scale with a M6th (or natural 6th).

Here's the D Dorian mode:

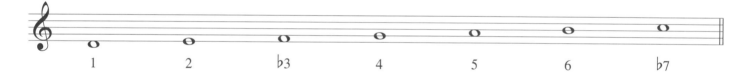

Here's the D Dorian mode in the eighth position:

D DORIAN MODE (EIGHTH POSITION)

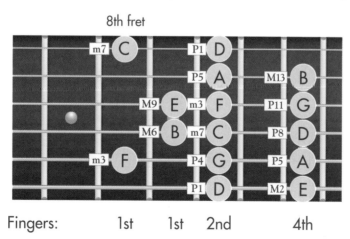

Keep in mind that any major scale you play by starting on the second scale degree will give you its Dorian mode.

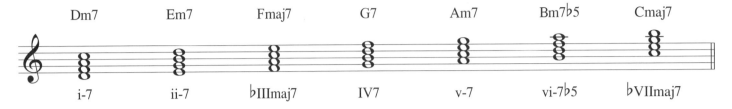

If you stack seventh chords on the Dorian mode, you will get its chord scale.

D Dorian Chord Scale

Dm7	Em7	Fmaj7	G7	Am7	Bm7♭5	Cmaj7
i-7	ii-7	♭IIImaj7	IV7	v-7	vi-7♭5	♭VIImaj7

You will also notice that the chord scale for D Dorian is the same as C major but starting from the second scale degree of the latter. So, the first chord in the D Dorian chord scale is a i-7, etc.

Below is a chord progression in the key of D Dorian. Try recording it and then jamming over it in the key of D Dorian (or C major). Here's where the blues scale and pentatonic extensions come in handy, because, as mentioned, the blues scale that was outlined previously has all the same notes as the Dorian scale, so you can play D blues over this progression.

Conversely, you can also play the D Dorian/blues scale with its pentatonic extensions over chord changes in the key of C major. The only difference is, when you are comfortable playing in D Dorian/blues over D Dorian chord changes, there are certain notes that sound good when ending a phrase on them. But, if playing D Dorian/blues over C major changes, those same notes will have a totally different flavor, so your phrasing and melodies would have to be adjusted for the flavor of the chord changes under them.

It may sound complicated, but if you just let your ears do the walking, you will know what works and what doesn't. Once again, listening is the key.

D Dorian Progression

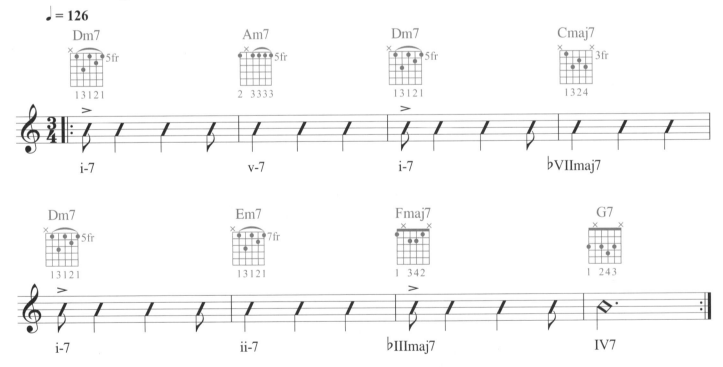

Dorian Flavor

The Dorian mode has almost a light minor flavor to it. It's a "sunset" scale against a dark blue sky, but not too dark. Listen to the atmosphere of the scale and how the notes work with it, and invest your attention in the atmosphere more than the fingerings of the scale.

Phrygian Mode: Third Mode of the Major Scale

So, in short, if you play a C major scale from E to E (the third degree of the C major scale), you are playing the E **Phrygian mode**. If you isolated the E Phrygian mode, the scale degrees would be 1–♭2–♭3–4–5–♭6–♭7. The Phrygian mode can also be called a minor scale with a m2 (or lowered 2nd).

Reflecting on the circle of 5ths, the key of E has four sharps in it: F♯, C♯, G♯, and D♯. So, an E scale with 1–♭2–♭3–4–5–♭6–♭7 (all natural notes) is the Phrygian mode.

E PHRYGIAN MODE (10TH POSITION)

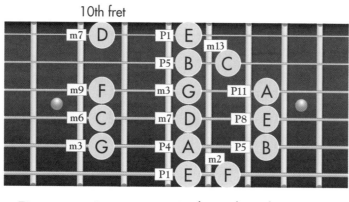

Fingers: 1st   2nd   3rd   4th

E Phrygian Chord Scale

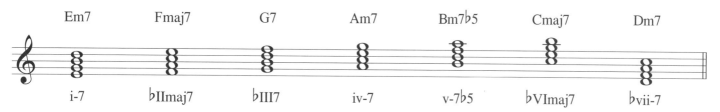

Em7	Fmaj7	G7	Am7	Bm7♭5	Cmaj7	Dm7
i-7	♭IImaj7	♭III7	iv-7	v-7♭5	♭VImaj7	♭vii-7

Following is a chord progression in the key of E Phrygian. You will notice that there are some tension notes on the chords that are not in the previous stacked seventh chord scale. The reason they work is because they are not outside of the E Phrygian scale and they sound OK. Any scale tones can be added to a chord as long as they sound like what you are looking for. This can open up a whole new set of chord flavors to your progressions.

Also, if I was playing over a chord progression in the key of E Phrygian, I might hover around D Dorian/blues. They are the same thing, but I know the Dorian mode all over the neck, in any key. The fretboard lights up for me when I associate anything with Dorian/blues. I might just do this to create neck awareness, but would accent and phrase notes in the D Dorian mode I'm using in a very different way so that they sound appropriate to my ear in the E Phrygian mode.

In the E Phrygian progression below, notice that the time signature is a composite time signature. The actual time signature is 7/8 but the pulse of the bars is 4+3. Also notice the downstrokes and upstrokes I added under the staff. These indicate the strumming direction.

E Phrygian Progression

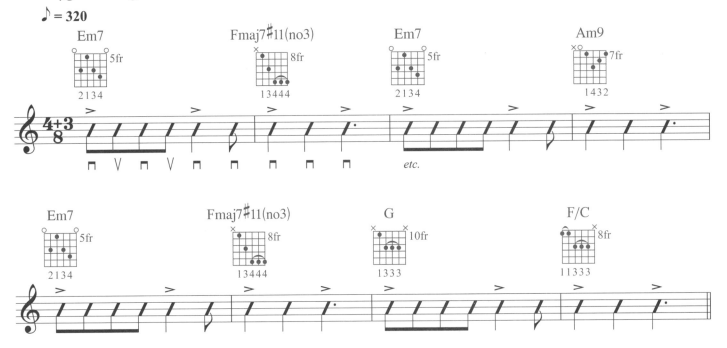

Phrygian Flavor

Listen carefully to the atmosphere of the Phrygian tonality and memorize it. You may find Phrygian to be sort of an exotic-sounding scale; it's like a cool desert landscape in Egypt. Try writing your own progressions in this key.

Lydian Mode: Fourth Mode of the Major Scale

The **Lydian mode** is a major scale with a raised 4th, or A4. Below is F Lydian:

F LYDIAN MODE (OPEN POSITION)

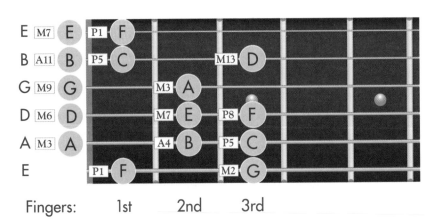

F Lydian Chord Scale

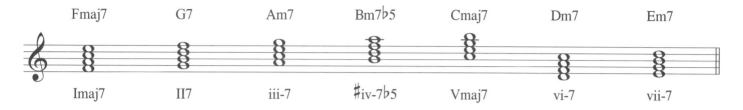

Try writing several progressions in the Lydian tonality and dig into the quality of the Lydian atmosphere.

Mixolydian Mode: Fifth Mode of the Major Scale

The **Mixolydian mode** is a major scale with a lowered 7th (also named m7, or dominant 7th). Below is the G Mixolydian mode:

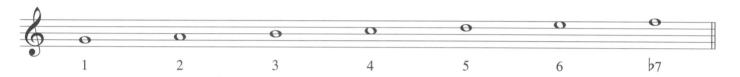

G MIXOLYDIAN MODE (FIRST POSITION)

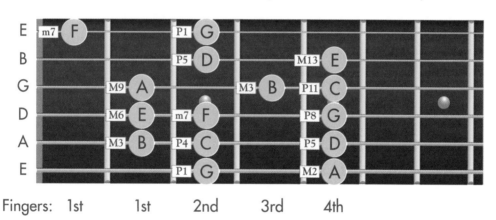

Fingers: 1st   1st   2nd   3rd   4th

G Mixolydian Chord Scale

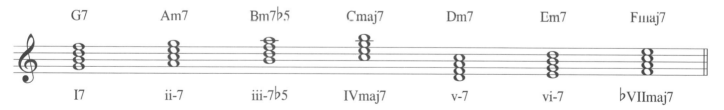

Try writing several progressions in the Mixolydian tonality and dig into the quality of the Mixolydian atmosphere. This scale is the tonality you perhaps hear most in pop and country music.

Aeolian Mode: Sixth Mode of the Major Scale

The **Aeolian mode** is also referred to as "pure minor" or "natural minor." It's the sixth scale degree (mode) of the major scale and is a major scale with a lowered 3rd, 6th, and 7th (or m3, m6, and m7). Below is the A Aeolian mode:

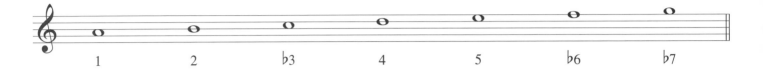

A AEOLIAN MODE (THIRD POSITION)

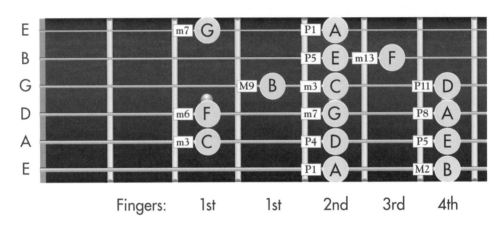

A Aeolian Chord Scale

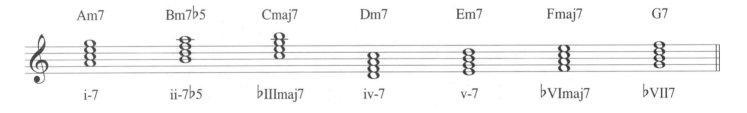

Try writing several progressions in the Aeolian tonality and dig into the quality of the Aeolian atmosphere. This is the scale that creates the dark, brooding tonality that is found in rock and other dramatic music.

Locrian Mode: Seventh Mode of the Major Scale

The **Locrian mode** is the scale that starts on the seventh degree of the major scale. It's a minor scale with a lowered 2nd and 5th, or m2 and d5. Its scale degrees are 1–m2–m3–4–d5–m6–m7. Below is the B Locrian mode:

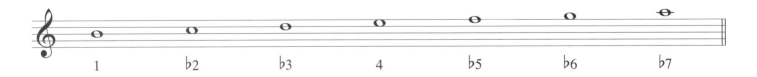

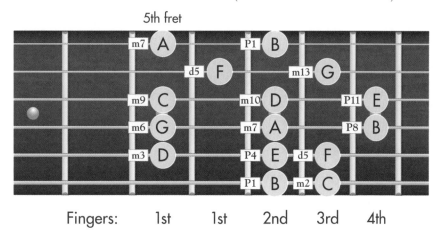

B Locrian Chord Scale

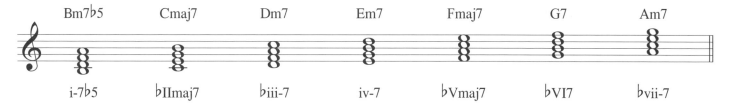

Try writing several progressions in the Locrian tonality and dig into the quality of the Locrian atmosphere. This is not a very common tonality; it's sort of Phrygian's ugly twin or a minor scale that grew up in a really rough neighborhood.

Additional Chord Tensions

The question arises: "How do I know what other tensions (notes) I can put in a chord so it works in the key I'm in?" And it's a good question. The answer is: any diatonic note within the scale.

For instance, if we were in the key of C major, you could technically apply any note in the scale to the chord. Since the scale degrees of a C major scale are 1–2–3–4–5–6–7, you can add these notes and their octaves to the chord. Obviously, you have to find what sounds good for the situation and also find the best voicings for them on the guitar.

Here are the various types of C chords that would work:

C, C2, Csus4, C6, C(6/9), Cmaj7, Cmaj9, Cmaj11, Cmaj13, C(add9, 11), etc.

If you were to add tensions to the ii-7 chord, Dm7, and since those tensions would be based on the Dorian mode (1–2–♭3–4–5–6–♭7), some of the tensions you could add to a D- chord would be:

Dm, Dm6, Dm7, Dm9, Dm11, Dm13, Dm(6/9), etc.

Here is a C major chord scale stacked in 3rds, with every available note tension on each of the scale's chord degrees:

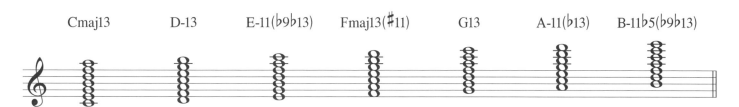

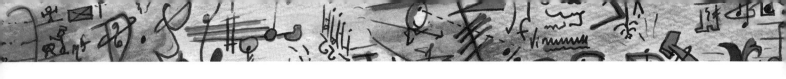

OTHER SCALES

Obviously, there are more scales than the major, minor, pentatonic, and their modes. Below are some of the more common scales that are not associated, note for note, with the major scale. These are all based in the key of C. Of course, there are a plethora of scales within music. Any string of notes can be considered a scale.

Harmonic Minor Scale

The **harmonic minor scale** is closely associated with the natural minor scale, with one exception: the harmonic minor scale has a raised 7th, or major 7th.

C Harmonic Minor

It gets very interesting when you create a chord scale around this scale by stacking 3rds to make seventh chords.

C Harmonic Minor Chord Scale

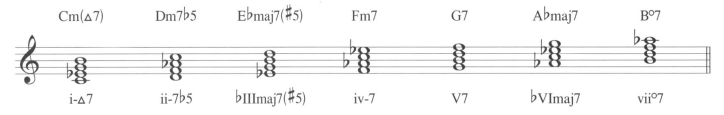

The modes of any scale are created the same way as the modes of the major scale. This is when it really starts to get interesting, because each mode of the harmonic minor scale sounds as vastly different from each other as the modes of the major scale.

	HARMONIC MINOR MODES	
1	Harmonic minor	Major scale with m3 and m6
2	Locrian ♮6	Minor scale with m2, d5, and M6
3	Ionian ♯5	Major scale with A5
4	Dorian ♯4	Minor scale with A4 and M6
5	Phrygian dominant	Minor scale with m2 and M3
6	Lydian ♯2	Major scale with A2 and A4
7	Locrian diminished ♭4	Minor scale with m2, d4, d5, and d7

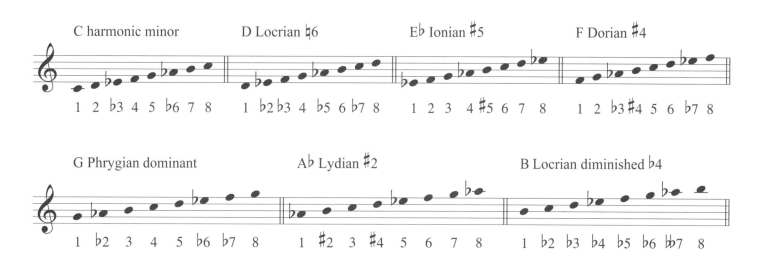

C harmonic minor   D Locrian ♮6   E♭ Ionian ♯5   F Dorian ♯4

1 2 ♭3 4 5 ♭6 7 8   1 ♭2 ♭3 4 ♭5 6 ♭7 8   1 2 3 4 ♯5 6 7 8   1 2 ♭3 ♯4 5 6 ♭7 8

G Phrygian dominant   A♭ Lydian ♯2   B Locrian diminished ♭4

1 ♭2 3 4 5 ♭6 ♭7 8   1 ♯2 3 ♯4 5 6 7 8   1 ♭2 ♭3 ♭4 ♭5 ♭6 ♭♭7 8

These are some pretty far-out and exotic-sounding scales. As you can imagine, you can create all sorts of different tonalities and melodic dimensions by using the various chord scales associated with the modes of the harmonic minor scale. Try fooling around with writing progressions based on this tonality.

Melodic Minor Scale

Traditionally in classical music, to play the **melodic minor scale**, you raise the sixth and seventh notes of the natural minor scale by a half step as you go up the scale, and then return to the natural minor as you go down the scale. The notes of the ascending C melodic minor scale are: C–D–E♭–F–G–A–B–C. The notes of the descending C melodic minor scale are: C–D–E♭–F–G–A♭–B♭–C (the C natural minor scale).

The variations of this scale in its ascent and descent are usually practiced more in traditional classical music. When I use the melodic minor scale, it's usually as the natural minor scale with a M6 and M7. Very cool sound.

Melodic Minor Modes

Try writing out the melodic minor chord scale stacked in 3rds to make seventh chords and use those chords in various progressions. Try doing this with all its modes, too!

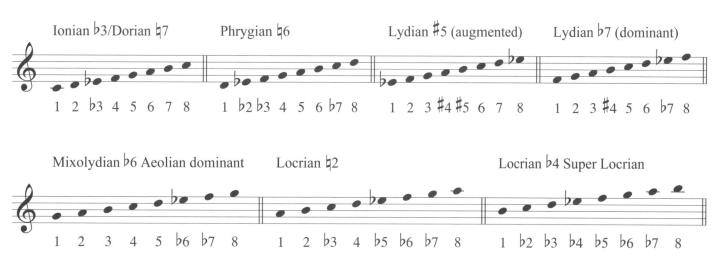

Ionian ♭3/Dorian ♮7   Phrygian ♮6   Lydian ♯5 (augmented)   Lydian ♭7 (dominant)

1 2 ♭3 4 5 6 7 8   1 ♭2 ♭3 4 5 6 ♭7 8   1 2 3 ♯4 ♯5 6 7 8   1 2 3 ♯4 5 6 ♭7 8

Mixolydian ♭6 Aeolian dominant   Locrian ♮2   Locrian ♭4 Super Locrian

1 2 3 4 5 ♭6 ♭7 8   1 2 ♭3 4 ♭5 ♭6 ♭7 8   1 ♭2 ♭3 ♭4 ♭5 ♭6 ♭7 8

For the remainder of the scales, experiment with the following:

1. Write them out in notation on the staff, in every key

2. Learn them in at least one position on the neck

3. Write out all their modes and name them based on their altered notes

4. Build four-note chord scales out of all their modes

5. Build several new chords on the guitar for each of the chords in the chord scale

6. Create various progressions in each of their modes and vary the tempo, time signature, etc.

7. Record the chord changes (bass and drums are optional but really help), then solo your butt off over each mode

Diminished Scale

The **diminished scale** is an eight-note (octatonic) scale that is built by alternating whole and half steps from any root note. There are two diminished scales in modern music, the fully diminished and dominant diminished (or half-diminished) scales. Though they share a name, each scale is used to outline different chords in your solos. You can use the dominant diminished scale to solo over seventh chords, and the other is used to solo over diminished seventh chords.

Each scale uses a different combination of whole and half steps. Fully diminished alternates whole and half steps, while dominant diminished alternates half and whole steps. Each scale brings a unique sound to diminished seventh and dominant seventh chords in your solos. And it's a good idea to keep both scales in your back pocket for some tasty improvised notes.

C Diminished Scale

Altered Scale

The **altered scale** is the seventh mode of the melodic minor scale (1–♭2–♯2–3–♭5–♯5–♭7), which means that it is like playing A♭ melodic minor but starting from the note G. The altered scale is used to solo over dominant seventh chords, both in major and minor keys. The altered scale contains all four of the common altered notes (♭9, ♯9, ♭5, and ♯5), which are used to create tension over the underlying chord when applying this scale to a soloing situation.

You can create scales based on anything from two to 12 notes. Imagine all the combinations of colors and tonalities you can get by creating chord scales and modes from them. And that's not including getting into microtone pitches!

Here is a handful of scales to play around with:

EVEN MORE SCALES	
Arabian	1–2–3–4–♭5–♭6–♭7
Gypsy minor (Byzantine, Double Harmonic)	1–♭2–3–4–5–♭6–7
Hungarian	1–♭3–3–♯4–5–6–♭7
Persian	1–♭2–3–4–♭5–♭6–7
Neapolitan minor	1–♭2–♭3–4–5–♭6–7
Enigmatic	1–♭2–3–♯4–♯5–♯6–7
Lydian diminished	1–2–♭3–♯4–5–6–7

HEXATONIC SCALES

Hawaiian	1–2–♭3–5–6–7
Whole Tone	1–2–3–♯4–♯5–♭7

PENTATONIC SCALES

Balinese	1–♭2–♭3–5–♭6
Japanese	1–♭2–4–5–♭6

IN CLOSING

In closing, this book is far from being comprehensive in regard to music theory, although it should give you enough to chew on for a while. If you understand all this and it actually excites you, the Internet is a virtually infinite information highway for exploring this stuff—deep enough to give yourself a harmonic hernia.

Having said that, if you can learn the basic principals in this book, you will no longer be musically illiterate, and you will find that communicating with other musicians, writing music, playing music, and your sense of esteem and confidence will be greatly enhanced. And I can only hope for that for you. That's why I created it.

Enjoy!
And thanks… really!

Steve Vai

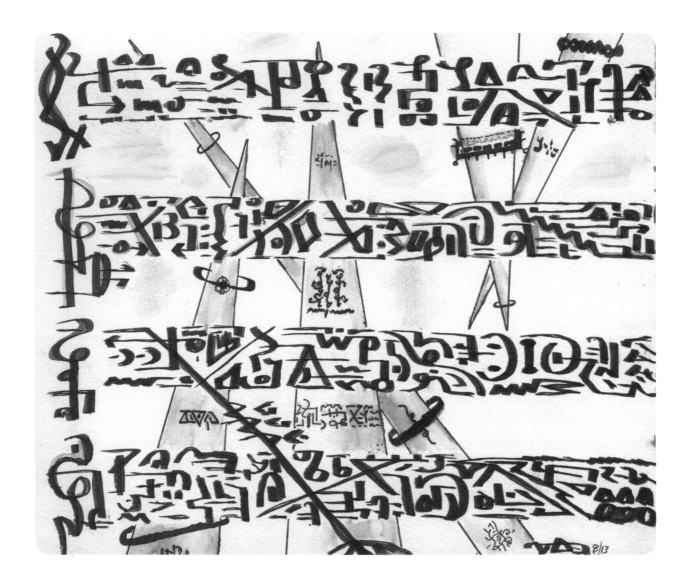

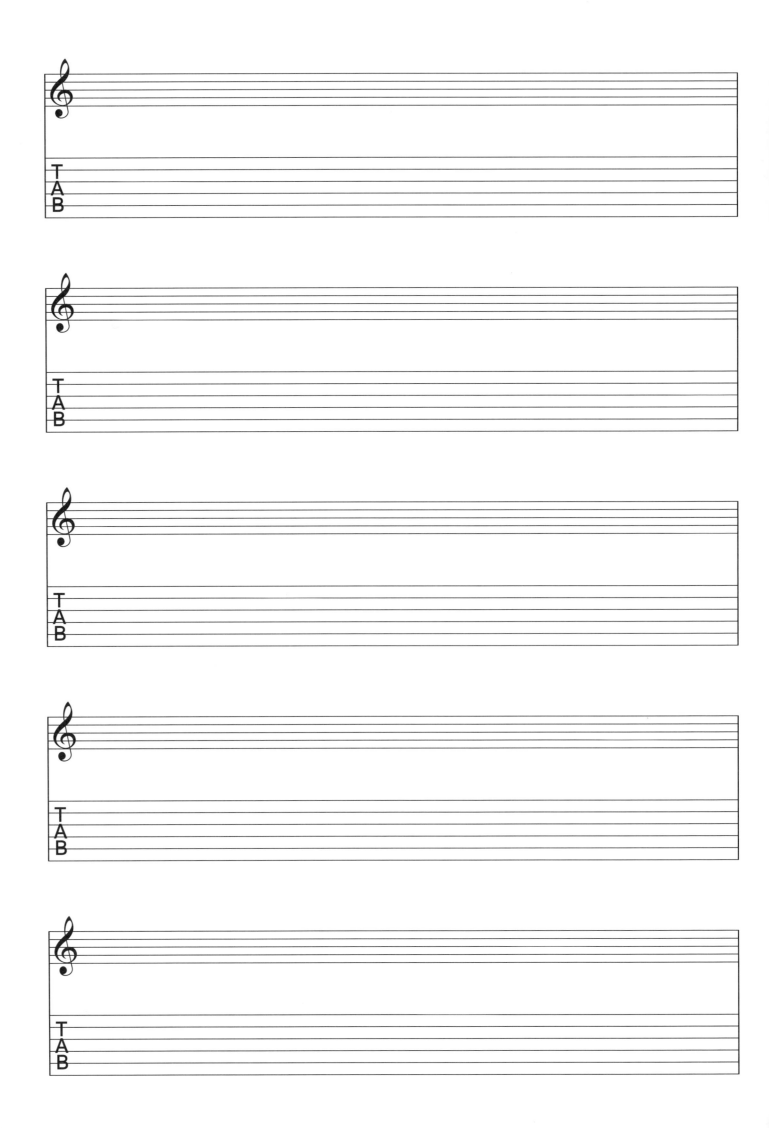

MORE OUTSTANDING PUBLICATIONS FROM
STEVE VAI

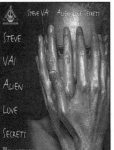

THE STORY OF LIGHT

INCLUDES TAB *The Story of Light* is the second installment in the *Real Illusions* planned trilogy, a "multi-layered melange based on the amplified mental exaggerations of a truth-seeking madman who sees the world through his own distorted perceptions." Play every epic note on Vai's 2012 release with these authentic transcriptions. Includes the title track and: Book of the Seven Seals • Creamsicle Sunset • Gravity Storm • John the Revelator • The Moon and I • Mullach a'tSí • No More Amsterdam • Racing the World • Sunshine Electric Raindrops • and more.
00110385 Guitar Recorded Versions...........$22.99

THE ULTRA ZONE

INCLUDES TAB On this album that the *All Music Guide* calls "an amazing exhibition of six-string talent," guitar virtuoso Steve Vai pays tribute to his mentor Frank Zappa on the song "Frank" and to Stevie Ray Vaughan on "Jibboom." This songbook also includes a special 8-page color section of photos and illustrations, and 11 more songs from the CD transcribed in notes & tab: Asian Sky • The Blood & Tears • Fever Dream • Here I Am • I'll Be Around • Lucky Charms • Oooo • The Silent Within • The Ultra Zone • and more.
00690392 Guitar Recorded Versions...........$19.95

INSTRUCTION

GUITAR WORLD PRESENTS STEVE VAI'S GUITAR WORKOUT

INCLUDES TAB Since its appearance in *Guitar World* in 1990, Vai's intensive guitar regimen has been the Holy Grail for serious players. Here is the lesson that shaped a generation of guitarists. Vai sat down with guitarist/transcriber Dave Whitehill and outlined his practice routine for the January 1990 issue of *Guitar World*. Never before had a guitarist given such an in-depth explanation of his musical exercise regimen. It became a must-have for guitarists. Many of the players interviewed in GW have cited it as an influence on their development as guitarists. Here's a chance to experience the workout in its original form and to learn some of the things Vai has done to develop his formidable chops and remarkable music vocabulary.

In this book, Steve Vai reveals his path to virtuoso enlightenment with two challenging guitar workouts - one 10-hour and one 30-hour - which include scale and chord exercises, ear training, sight-reading, music theory, and much more. These comprehensive workouts are reprinted by permission from *Guitar World* magazine.
00119643..$14.99

STEVE VAI - GUITAR STYLES & TECHNIQUES

INCLUDES TAB

by Jeff Perrin
Signature Licks
Play along with the actual backing tracks from "Passion and Warfare" and "Sex & Religion," specially modified by Steve Vai himself! Learn the secrets behind a guitar virtuoso then play along like the pro himself. Songs: The Animal • Answers • For the Love of God • Rescue Me or Bury Me • The Riddle • Sex & Religion • Still My Bleeding Heart • Touching Tongues.
00673247 Book/CD Pack $22.95

ALIEN LOVE SECRETS: NAKED VAMPS

INCLUDES TAB

by Steve Vai and Wolf Marshall
Signature Licks
Learn the secrets behind this guitar virtuoso then play along like Vai himself with the actual backing tracks from *Alien Love Secrets*! Songs include: Bad Horsie • The Boy from Seattle • Die to Live • Juice • Tender Surrender • more.
00695223 Book/CD Pack $22.95

FIRE GARDEN: NAKED VAMPS

INCLUDES TAB

by Steve Vai and Wolf Marshall
Signature Licks
This unique package lets guitarists learn Steve Vai's style and techniques by playing along with the actual backing tracks from *Fire Garden*! Features 8 songs: Aching Hunger • Blowfish • Brother • The Crying Machine • Little Alligator • Taurus Bulba • There's a Fire in the House • Warm Regards.
00695166 Book/CD Pack $22.95

THE ULTRA ZONE: NAKED VAMPS

INCLUDES TAB

by Wolf Marshall
Signature Licks
Learn the secrets behind the signature sounds of this guitar virtuoso, and then play along with the *actual backing tracks* from *The Ultra Zone* - mixed and produced by Vai himself! In this unique book/CD pack, Wolf Marshall teaches you everything you need to know to play exactly like Steve. Songs include: The Blood & Tears • I'll Be Around • Jibboom • The Silent Within • The Ultra Zone • Voodoo Acid • Windows to the Soul.
00695684 Book/CD Pack $22.95

STEVE VAI - GUITAR PLAY-ALONG VOLUME 193

INCLUDES TAB The Guitar Play-Along Series will help you play your favorite songs quickly and easily! Just follow the tab, listen to the audio to hear how the guitar should sound, and then play along using the separate backing tracks. The melody and lyrics are also included in the book in case you want to sing, or to simply help you follow along. The audio is available online for download or streaming, and it is enhanced so you can adjust the recording to any tempo without changing pitch!

8 songs: The Attitude Song • The Crying Machine • Die to Live • For the Love of God • I Would Love To • Sunshine Electric Raindrops • Tender Surrender • Touching Tongues.
00156028 Book/Online Audio......................$19.99

DVDs

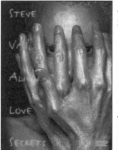

ALIEN LOVE SECRETS

DVD Now on DVD, the full-length matching video to one of his albums. This video includes full performances of all seven songs from *Alien Love Secrets*. The performance features Steve's power trio of Robbie Harrington on bass, Chris Frazier on drums, and of course Steve himself on guitar. This unique performance video format allows you a special view into both Steve's guitar playing, as well as the creative musical mood and aura of each song. Featured songs include: Juice • Die to Live • and the grand finale power guitar ballad "Tender Surrender." 40 minutes.
00320540 DVD...$19.95

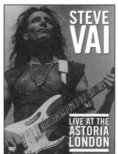

LIVE AT THE ASTORIA LONDON

DVD

Favored Nations
Steve Vai, Billy Sheehan, Tony MacAlpine, Virgil Donati, Dave Weiner - Live in London! If you couldn't be at the Astoria for these extraordinary shows, then this DVD is the next best thing: an unbelievable concert video featuring backstage and behind-the-scenes footage, interviews, band biographies, a Vai discography, rehearsal coverage, and 21 songs - nearly 4 HOURS of footage! Also features Dolby Digital 5.1 Surround Sound, PCM Stereo, Audio Commentary, and Instant Chapter Access to Songs.
00320433 DVD...$19.95

HAL•LEONARD®
www.halleonard.com